WILLOUGHBY COLLEGE (1865.)

To the Students of the past and present, of those public life, labors and prayers, this

New Hampshire Conference Seminary and Female College (1875.)

Seminaries, to which the Author has given all his volume is affectionately dedicated.

Infidelity Answered

BY

The Father-God

AND

His Family.

BY REV. JOHN B. ROBINSON, A. M.,
President of New-Hampshire Conference Seminary and
Female College.

BOSTON.
FOR SALE BY JAMES P. MAGEE,
38 Bromfield Street.
1875.

Entered, according to Act of Congress, in the year 1875,
BY J. B. ROBINSON,
in the Office of the Librarian of Congress, at Washington.

PREFACE.

Much error, claiming to be both scientific and religious, is neither. True science and religion discover the fallacy and reject these spurious claims. Such, for illustration, is Darwin's *Origin of Species*. It is a book of 437 pages. Each page, upon a fair average, has ten probabilities and possibilities, and each of these hypotheticals has no more than fifty per cent, or a half chance of certainty. His argument is so conducted that each proposition must stand or fall upon the validity of all that precede it combined. Then with 437 pages and ten half chances on each page, if it is desirable to know the fraction of truth in the final assertion on the last page, we have only to regard that there are 10 X 437 half chances, in other words that one half must be raised to the 4370th power. The numerator, which would be one unit, would represent the only chance in Darwin's favor, while the denominator, minus one, will represent the chances against him. But that denominator becomes overwhelming ; it would require a round number of more than *fourteen hundred digits* to express it, and a blackboard of *one hundred and twenty feet* in length to write it, allowing one inch to a figure. Thus does human reason, diverging but a little from the straight line of truth, finally separate from it into infinite distances of error.

Thus the author of the *Mode of Man's Immortality*, a book just published at Indianapolis, makes but a slight departure from Orthodoxy and reaches finally very erroneous conclusions. When we leave God and the Bible to follow human theories, however ingenious, we tend surely to the lowest horizon of error. The following pages indirectly combat the errors of the books just alluded to, but their higher mission is to assist in directing the doctrines and faith of many a seeker of truth in these fields.

Many standard authors have been consulted, and their thoughts sometimes used, in passing, without special credit, except as now named. Among authors thus consulted are Hagenback, Watson, Angus, Butler, Clark, Henry, and Bishops Clark, Thompson, and Kingsley, to all of whom obligation is hereby expressed.

J. B. R.

TILTON, N. H., Jan. 1, 1875.

Truth crushed to earth will rise again,
The eternal years of God are hers;
But error, writhing in her chain,
Falls dead among her worshipers.

CONTENTS.

PART I.

THE FATHER—GOD.

CHAPTER I.

CHAPTER II.

CHAPTER III.

CHAPTER IV.

CHAPTER V.

CHAPTER VI.

PART II.

THE FATHER—GOD'S FAMILY.

CHAPTER. I.

CHAPTER II.

CHAPTER III.

CHAPTER IV.

CHAPTER V.

CHAPTER VI.

ILLUSTRATIONS.

PART I.

THE FATHER-GOD.

CHAPTER I.

The God of Nature.

When Sir William Thompson would inaugurate the British Association with the announcement, that earth may have been originally peopled from the remnants of former worlds, through seed transported by meteors and comets' tails, it is time Nature, History, Revelation and God should rebuke him.

When Darwin in a well bound book, gravely suggests the probability that man started by spontaneous generation from the monad of the puddle, and grew by a series of developments to man the human, it is time such a wild lunatic should be caged in the asylums of public pity and contempt. Such a morbid growth of free fancy, in France, that hot-bed of all bloated and perverted imagination, and such a free publication of obnoxious books as now floods Christendom, will be sufficient apology for our efforts to display truth and vindicate it. We gather into comprehensible form such *a posteriori* proofs of GOD as may occur. And first we go to

NATURE.

The modern infidel or atheist, descendant of the "fool" of David's day, pretends to have a creed which demands an adverse, negative faith, infinitely beyond the faith of Abraham. These creeds he thrusts before the world in opposition to the mighty proofs of DEITY, which rise to heaven, sink to hell, take the wings of the morning and fly through the Universe;—proofs which penetrate through and through existence, expanding and germinating the grain of mustard-seed faith into the evident certainty of a GOD everywhere.

The Atheist with creeds which for labored effort in their birth are like the twelve labors of Hercules, for goading of spirit in their rearing and perpetuation are like the tortures of a Prometheus, cannot, when he denies God, account for even a grain of mustard seed.

In fact there are no sincere atheists; for those so called are only experimenting upon human credence to deduce the impossible. The problem is absurd. The so-called atheist is either tempted into deception or is an essential hypocrite, for he misrepresents himself. He does not believe his own theory, in his life or his death. Yet his theory may be his subterfuge until death, when the proofs are transferred into eternity. Neither angels nor devils are atheists, though both are acquainted with immortality. Man alone is the doubting creature. Nor is such drizzling faith peculiar to the deaf, dumb, and blind, as we might suppose, but it pertains to men of ears and eyes, of leisure and luxury. Atheism becomes a morbid and stupefying contagion—fatal, if not checked. To its prevention or remedy all around us, let us bestir ourselves.

1. *Assume the truth of Atheism in nature.* Then the rational mind expects, but seeks in vain for certain circumstances in conformity with it. If plan and power and authority were wanting to the world around us, we should rationally expect order to cease and chaos to ensue. Gravity would cease to

hold matter in its arms, and matter of earth, or planet, or star would fall wildly into space; light of day would yield to hopeless, eternal night; warmth would give place to cheerless, perpetual cold; and, with the dissolution of matter, would come the dissolution of all life, animal and vegetable; and organism would tumble into total destruction, since no uniform law could possibly exist in the absence of a law-giver. Spirit must also cease; and all that is orderly, beautiful or existent, in any form, must recede into one hopeless, helpless, chaotic, eternal oblivion. The last star would flicker and set forever, and the last Spirit would dissolve in night. What a dire sequence would be realized, were atheism true! But the very reverse of all these hypotheses is the daily wonder of this world. Every hour a myriad of mysteries, like a universe of miracles, is poured into the faith of man.

2. FORCE *or* POWER *all would agree, is an attribute of Ga od.* Weakness is human, and yet weakness is limited power. Inertia, or absence of power, extant in all things, as mind, soul, body, so as to disperse all in dark, perpetual death, would be a sign of truth in atheism. In such case, however the Atheist would never live to make the observation.

But as inertia is limited, by law, to matter, the limitation is the sign of a God. It requires power to hold matter grouped into worlds, to hold worlds by fixed laws and roll them with undeviating regularity. Since power is diffused through thousands of stirring forms, and numberless life, since power is in the wave, and the cloud, and the wind, and the volcano, and the earthquake, and the gentle fire, and the pure snow-flake, and the growing tree, and the soaring bird, and the raging beast, and the sporting fish, all subject to fixed law, a God must have diffused that power, and limited, and delegated and fixed it. And the power of the God must be infinitely greater than the sum of all delegated and diffused powers. That all manifest power is put forth in obedience to laws, indicates all *wisdom* as an attribute of God; that these laws produce happiness to life proves *goodness* as an attribute of God; and that violated laws have penalties, indicates *justice* in Deity. Thus the very nature of Deity is manifest in Nature.

3. *The law of attraction supposes a God.* If polytheism were true and each planet had its special divinity, then repulsion would often be the disposition of planet to planet. And the war of forces

which polytheism would bring in the dissolution of the universe, would be as calamitous as the theory of atheism, which never could have permitted the existence of a universe. See a Newton, driven by the plague of desolation from Cambridge, to the manor house at Woolsthorpe. He is the John—the Revelator on the Patmos of vision in the kingdom of Nature. He is about to have a Revelation of a GOD. It was autumn. He sat under a tree of the garden. The vision begins. An apple falls. Thought rises. Thought grows out of thought. Fact links to fact. All bodies near earth fall to it. Earth rises to sun, and holds out an arm of support to sister planet. Planets live in families. Families of planets are bound to other such families. Not one is isolated. The enlarging plan is linked from deep cavern to high mountain, from high mountain to distant moon, from distant moon to primary world, from primary world to bright sun, from bright sun to the burning throne of a JEHOVAH. One has justly said. "In the author of the *Principia*, one arose, who, grasping the master key of the universe, and treading its celestial paths, opened up to the human intellect, the stupendous realities of the material world, and, in the unrolling of its harmonies, gave to the human heart a new song to the goodness, wisdom and majesty of the all-creating, all-sustaining, all-perfect GOD." Such was the vision of Newton, and such is the sublime lesson of gravitation or attraction.

4. *Regular succession in nature indicates a God.* When the human mind discovers that about it all things exist by the uniform operation of natural laws, that moment DEITY must be admitted. The very bird and beast have discovered that day and night, summer and winter, come and go in order. It never occurred to the atheist that when order reigns, chance is banished and GOD is.

5. *Existing truth supposes God.* "What is truth?" asked Pilate. "There's nothing true but heaven," sings the poet. We cannot believe that, abstract truth itself would exist, unless a DEITY first make abstract truth. Truth is simply the exponent of a GOD. Without Him it cannot be asserted that even axioms are true. Without GOD we cannot affirm two multiplied by two equal four, nor that "the whole is equal to the sum of all its parts." Banish GOD and nature is a lie, mind is banished, law is banished, and all axioms, and all truth; all the primary conceptions of mathematics

and of mind sink into inextricable chaos. Hence all the profound and beautiful propositions in Geometry, all the ever certain gradations of quantity in Calculus, first had birth in a divine mind. Thus, the square of the hypothenuse of a right-angled triangle is equal to the sum of the squares of the other two sides, which forced the "*Eureka*" of joy from old Pythagoras, was really the problem of a GOD. Without GOD the *reductio ad absurdum* would be as good truth as the *Binomial Theorem.* Polyedrons and cubes, spheres and cylinders, must die when DEITY dies. The infinities of mathematics depend on the infinities of GOD.

6. *Every part of Astronomy makes a God a positive necessity.* The naked eye of David "considered the heavens," and his heart bounded out to GOD. The telescope, though voiceless, is a most eloquent preacher of Theism. The spectroscope comes with its great load of testimony, and tells of the constituents of the heavenly bodies, and indentifies their iron, oxygen, hydrogen with that of earth thus proving sister worlds blood of our blood and flesh of our flesh, as to constituents; this makes the GOD of the stars our GOD. The atheist must not look up, the meteors of night confound him. Luminous

foot-prints of God, walking in the sky, confront him everywhere. "Who made these?" is a question which leads to God. "Who upholds them?" It can only be an Almighty. "Who hurls them harmoniously into stupendous motion for ages?" The answer must be, only All-mighty power with Almighty wisdom. Where is the undevout astronomer? In the mad house. He is at home there. The intimation that lunacy comes from looking at the moon is an exploded theory; we recommend such gazing for a cure of the moral lunacy of atheism. Let me live where the stars spread out their potent formulas to reason. Let my soul look up when the sun showers beams of evidence. The poet holds up this mirror of God:

> "God of the rolling orbs!
> Thy name is written clearly bright
> In the warm day's unvarying blaze,
> Or evening's golden shower of light,
> For every fire that fronts the sun,
> And every spark that walks alone
> Around the utmost verge of heaven,
> Were kindled at thy burning throne."

7. *The Almanac publisher is indebted to a God for the accuracy and value of his book.* Since he can predict an eclipse, or the moment of the rising or set-

ting of the sun, moon or planet it is an evidence that a Being capable of moving these bodies governs them each moment. Almanacs are Revelations of God.

8. *Whence comes light but from God?* Is it from chaos and wild chance? It supposes both the luminous body and the transparent media. Swift as thought it leaps from its source and pours its lucid streams upon the world. Who can account for the phenomena unless upon the hypothesis that a God said "Let there be light and there was light?" Space is illuminated so that when the telescope peers into any path of ether, the path is lit up. Light fills the universe. Light is positive and must have an origin; darkness is negative and requires no other origin than the absence of God—than atheism made true. Human vision, spreading from the horizon of the east to the west, from north to south, and rounded up into the concave of the heavens is one ceaseless flood of testimony of the sublime Architect of Light bearing witness of Himself. Then the great cloud abyss of darkness flies; darkness cannot stay where God is, since "God is light."

"And never but in unapproached light,
Dwelt from eternity, dwelt then in thee,
Bright effluence of bright essence increate."

9. *Heat, a positive force of the universe, affirms a God.* Motion arrested is converted into heat. The anvil is warmed by the arrested stroke of the constant sledge. The same atheistical inertia which opposes motion, would also soon cool the ardor of the world, were not potent energies constantly feeding the exhausting caloric. So that, were there no GOD, instantly to the gloom of eternal night would be added the cheerlessness of eternal cold—nature in the cold death-sweat. Heat, an essential element to all life, attests its author GOD. From the distant sun, heat diffuses to the spaces at the benignant command of the Maker. Some of this reserve force is shut in the bowels of earth, raising its temperature, communicating to the ocean, lifting up the mountain by the earthquake and the volcano. The internal fire is in perfect control; gravity neutralizes its explosiveness and binds the earth in a unity.

10. *The rocky masonry of earth is certainly the work of a God.* Chance never planted the firm granite and the syenite as a key-stone arch around the in-

ternal fires. None but a God could have put above these the useful marble, the sandstones and the argillaceous clays, and protected the inexhaustible coals of the mine from the fires within. What substantial masonry is the globe! What a plan of design! What a splendid stepping-stone to the city of mansions! how guarded in its mathematical form against the crushing power of gravity!

11. *The Soil on the rocks is a token of divine Wisdom.* What were barren rocks for a habitation, were the whole surface polished and paved with the finest marble? It was not chance that fell upon the rocks and ground them to powder to make the layers of soils and clays. The mill of a God ground them, for benign purposes, in the ages. Let faithless man count the strata of the crust and examine their grand designs, let him dig into the deep mine and emerge with the gold and silver, and ask him if no profound plan lingers among the rocks. Ask Hugh Miller, as he gazes in astonishment at the writings on the natural rocks beneath us, if aught is there. He replies "Footprints of the Creator."

12. *Earth's uneven surface discloses God.* If the crust were perfectly level, of uniform rotundity, no land would appear. The waters would prevail over

all the surface. Earth were then one great deep. But the wisdom which elevated a part, and dipped out vast depressions elsewhere, is indubitable evidence of design. By these inequalities the ocean is confined safely within its shores; the plains and lowlands, full of rich loam, are leveled and convenient for cultivation; the hills are made to furnish essential soil for many productions; and the mountains are made the vast reservoirs of snow and rain, and the inducing cause of wind and variety. Diversified scenery is served, monotony is relieved, and man's love of the beautiful is fostered. There may be awful desolation in the mountain's top, but there the infant river is born, and there it laughs and sings and skips until its strength and size invite it down the mountain side. Thus have their birth the Nile, the Hoang Ho, the Volga, the Amazon and the great Mississippi. The same unevenness of surface leads out all the arms of ocean and builds up all inland lakes, makes the lands accessible by natural highways of water, and prepares for the commerce of the globe.

13. *God is in the clouds and the rain.* To test the strength of chance or of man let all other conditions be bestowed, but let the rain and the clouds

be withheld. Then what of life upon the earth? Drought and death must suddenly begin, as the cooling showers cease, until desolation reigns with no abatement. No man can change destiny, no fate can lift the water in the white cloud and fill the earth with joy. No power can rise aloft to spread out the cloud as a garment. It is the prerogative of a GOD to send the rains in their seasons, and to fill the rivers with leaping fountains. The evaporation which creates clouds sifts the salt back into ocean and brings only the pure mountain stream for universal use. This is Divine wisdom. It matters not if the cloud be congealed into the white snow that covers earth. Catch the flakes; apply the microscope; do you find chaos? No: the flakes fall down in symmetry, now like the bright wheel in the chariot of Elijah, now like the gorgeous chandeliers of St. Peter's, and now beautiful and rich as the array of a constellation of night. The snows flake is a part of GOD's mathematics, it is his winged manna, so pure, to feed faith and send it up above earth to where the crystals are formed by JEHOVAH's fingers in the white clou d.

14. *Vegetation is a God's handy work.* Give the atheist all the previous conditions and let him exert

his skill in the production of a vegetable, independent of God. He may make an artifical flower by borrowing the thought and the material from God; but it is a daub without life or growth, But see sprigs of grass arising out of clay! Now the blade rises into tender green. If this be a modification of the clod, it is a miracle; if not, it is a greater miracle. It is superhuman in perfection, in life, in continuance.

Again, I see from a small seed, radicle and plumule start for their destinations; from blade tobu d, from bud to flower, from flower to fruit, onward they go to perfection. What delicate fringes and hues adorn that flower! what nectarine sweets fill its cup! what delicious perfumes distil from its petals! The acorn falls, sinks in earth, but lo! soon peers the infant oak. It rises despite gravity, despite winds, despite change, and stands, ages after, monarch of the forest, hardened into solidity, venerable with age, magnificent in grandeur, pointing to the stars. Its rings refer back to the days of Richard the Lion-Hearted and to the Saxon Heptarchy. Is it chance? No. Design is in every leaf, and twig, and sap vescicle and fibre. No part can be. accident. A myriad of miracles make the Summer glorious; and amid the infinite variety there is no failure. Silently and slowly the vegetable world inspires the noxious carbon, eliminating the healthful oxygen. Thus the forest is a laboratory whose changes prepare for and invite animal life. The conceptions of man are impotent for such stupendous plans, and the weakness of man is too enervating for their execution.

No principle of order could ever make a leaf, for without God, inertia, darkness, chaos, and death is the order. The leaves and the forest cannot possibly be regarded as the absurd result of shaking up the elements by accident. If accident could act without Providence, the result must be "only evil continually". Or, is nature prankish and only making appearances to deceive us all, after first making credence susceptible to pranks and deception? Old Dame Nature must be a cruel mother to be making mental buffoons of her children.

> "There is not a plant, a tree, a leaf, a flower,
> But contains a folio volume."

And every word of this vast library of the vegetable world is inscribed with the motto, "There is one God."

15. *Animal forms denote a Creator.* What are

these creeping things? What are these well wrought masses of walking matter? What are these phantoms that swim? What are these flying phenomena? Nature is rising up in living forms. What prank is *this?* Is there not danger that in this tendency of things, the old earth itself will some day assume tusks and a proboscis and walk off with us all on its back? Let the atheist beware of that day, for the elephant may possibly become carnivorous in those unique changes!

Hark! I hear this animal life breathe: it moves. Now it sings, or twitters, or croaks, or neighs, or lows, or roars, or barks, or hisses, or coos, or brays, or bleats, or whistles. Now it moves: it walks, or runs, or skips, or swims, or soars, or leaps, or trots, or dances. Now it sleeps, or loves, or hates, or fights, or retreats, or shivers, or swelters, or laughs, or weeps. Now it builds houses, or hoards food, or immigrates, or eats, or drinks, or revels in society. Now it lives and now it dies. This is animal life. They are the profound lessons of design and of evident Deity around us: they are sermons to convince our faith in God. The fish comes with his fins and his air vescicles; the beast comes with his fur or hair or thick skin, with his sharp or flat teeth, as his wants require; with his hoofs or his claws, with his strong limbs for offensive, or his nimble ones for defensive use; the bird comes with his fairy feathers, and his light bones, all harmonious with his mode of existence; the ground mole, the worm, the eel, and the dwellers in caves come with their eyeless brows, thankful for deliverance from eyes which to them would be fatal; and these all have one lesson and voice, that of adaptation and providence.

Nay more; the very eye of an animal speaks of GOD. All its lenses, humors, coats, curtains, muscles, nerves, and its final vision mounting, seizing upon the phenomena of light until the very stars are photographed within us—all these are final arguments of a GOD. Every bone of the frame work, every muscle of the human cordage, every nerve of the animal telegraph system, every organ of the internal cavities, every meandering stream of crimson blood bespeaks creative skill.

16. *The air is an emblem of an invisible spirit.* "The wind bloweth where it listeth." The ocean of air with its balmy breezes and its potential storms has a significant eloquence. Now it bears up the soaring bird, now it dissipates the noxious smokes and vapors, now it buoys up the rain cloud, from the

ocean to the distant land, and now it gently seeks the lungs of every living thing to pour in its treasures of life. We may not see it, but we can hear its voice in the pines and the mulberry trees, and we can feel its power in the breath. Were the air mixed in a little different proportion, it would become "laughing gas" which would briefly intoxicate all, and hurry life into fearful brevity. If one more element of oxygen entered the formula, the whole atmosphere would become an irrespirable poison. Blessed is the man whose daily breath is not prepared by the Chemistry of atheism or of chance.

17. *The crowning proof of God is man.* He has the beautiful, upright form, the cheek of dimpled loveliness, the eye of fire and the brow of God-like mien. He has the supremacy over all animal life. For without a supreme head to govern, subdue and protect, all that is noble on earth must still tumble into disorder, strife and ruin. Man is not supreme because of his strength or prowess. The lion is bolder, the whale is larger and more formidable; the eagle soars higher, but man, full of intelligence, representing the very DEITY whose attributes are portrayed in nature, inherits authority

by the power of mind and spirit. His thoughts burn, his memories recover the lost, his judgments rest upon reason, his imaginations create, his passions rise and fall, his plans comprehend the mortal and the immortal. Man is not a God; but man's nobility elevates our conceptions of a God.

Man's hands are not modifications of animal limbs, but better; they grasp with firmness, delicacy and facility. Hands portend skill and progress; they lead to trades and professions which prove man's supremacy. Such hands, put upon the fore-arm of a beast without mind, must be worse than useless, a power for evil. Souls are the essential counterparts of hands. Were chance or accident to cause the horse and the man to exchange hand for hoof, then man's work would be revolutionized, he would become the mauling animal; but his hoofs would be subservient to no end in his economy and he would die for want of hands; while the horse would become the pawing animal, but he too would soon die for want of his hoofs. Fabled monsters combining the horse and the fish, or the man and the horse, are only fanciful, not real. Not the man alone who ascends the pulpit is a preacher of God, but all preach by their wonderful forms. Man preaches to himself; his body preaches to his soul, and the theme absorbs existence.

> "Dim miniature of greatness absolute !
> An heir of glory ! a frail child of dust !
> Helpless immortal ! insect infinite !
> A worm ! a GOD ! I tremble at myself,
> And in myself am lost."

But the atheist retreats from a living soul; it is the warm breath of a GOD. It is the most formidable and unaccountable mystery of the universe. Secured from infidelity and mortality, the soul stands defiant. It

> "Smiles
> At the drawn dagger, and defies its point,
> The stars shall fade away, the sun himself
> Grow dim with age, and Nature sink in years ;
> But thou shalt flourish in immortal youth ;
> Unhurt amid the war of elements,
> The wreck of matter, and the crush of worlds."

18. *Finally, the succcss of the entire plan is the highest possible test of its divine author.* Adaptation and harmony run up through all creation. The mighty plan is a success, and the scheme a unity, from the glow worm which sends a dim lustre but a few feet, up to the burning sun that kindles glory through all space, from the parental love that rescues infancy from want, up to the divine benevolence that

superintends the universal family, from the opportune autumn winds that shake from the trees the rich ripe fruit, to the law of gravitation that binds world to world. Such schisms as would result from polytheism do not mar the internal government. Horrid chaos does not brood eternally as it would under atheism, with no GOD to say, "Let there be light." This perfect adaptation, from the infinitely insignificant of the life we behold with a microscope up to the infinitely great which astonishes us under the telescope, together with the infinite variety that fills the spaces between these extremes, speak a universal, an omnipotent, a perfect, an ever present GOD, the Creator and Preserver. The work could not be accomplished by angels, it is too formidable; it could not be divided and shared by two or more divinities, it is too harmonious and perfect in such variety. It cannot be less than the one, undivided JEHOVAH of the Christian, for it would weary, and stagger and crush a limited GOD. It can not be the chance or accident of atheism, or the development of Darwinism, for that were the most illogical, unnatural, puesile, idiotic assum ptionof this most stupendous effect, namely a Nature without a cause!

Thus far we have taken the proofs of God wholly from Nature. But beware of Deism which admits one God, but denies Revelation and appeals to reason. This would be an appeal to darkness when light has come. Beyond Nature we may go and take the "lamp to our feet." For collateral evidences of these sublime proofs of God consult freely all the Philosophies, Astronomies, Chemistries, Zoölogies, Geologies, Botanies, Physiologies, Mental Philosophies, Natural Histories, Natural Theologies and Nature Charts in the world. They are all sparkling proofs and commentaries of the theme. "The Father God." May that leading truth uphold every heart, fixed as the mountains resting on the granite ribs of the globe.

CHAPTER II.

THE GOD OF HISTORY.

WHILE Nature preached a GOD, with the voice of thunder, History sends down the echo with the voice of other thunders. *Jehovah not only creates,*

JEHOVAH REIGNS.

Six thousand years that voice responsive has proclaimed the astonishing counterpart. *God is in history.*

On yonder distant raveled edge of time, man looms up from nothing and takes a subordinate dominion over the world. Over him still is some formidable power, some unmanageable, superhuman arm, which subdues and rules, rewards and punishes, creates and destroys. Hidden as eternity are the first periods of human life and national compact, unless GOD reveal. In courts of law and equity, the plaintiff and defendant are competent witnesses. The testimony of GOD begins in His Word. It is not "begging the question" if the Bible chronicles be taken as valid as other histories at least. In this manner we claim credibility for the Bible as a History. Like other histories, but with multiplied certainty, it is corroborated, as to evidence on matters of fact. When History does appear, then also DEITY appears, creating light, creating plan, and deriving superhuman results.

Wars with powerful decision exalt or demolish nations, yet evidently some power apart from chance or generalship militates in battle. GOD takes a grand and solemn walk down the ages, and although the general reader is presented with the actions of heroes and statesmen, yet the serious and candid student discovers everywhere an extraordinary prescience displayed in the wonderful combinations of the past and present, embracing more than the age of man, and swaying nations hostile, and men of mutual enmity into common channels. No wonder heroes were deified and called gods, for they were simply the exponents of the will and work of the great GOD. By the heathen without spiritual eyes, the omnipotent, invisible arm was attributed to the visible man, the clay puppet. History becomes more than a political chess-board.

From the perturbations, and irregular motions and strange departures of Uranus, astronomers said there must be another planet beyond. From this mighty effect of some invisible world lying far off in space, men were moved to sweep the sky with the great telescope of Berlin, and, behold! the planet Neptune was seen out in space, making his grand march around the sun once in one hundred and sixty-four years. So in the political sky, these men who loom up as stars of fortune and fame often reel and sink, retreat and tumble into oblivion, or rise in accelerated splendor and move with unaccountable velocity. Pharaoh's chariot wheels go heavily and whirl to earth until the sea is their tomb. Sennacherib leading his host, disappears in death. Xerxes and his superb army are dissolved like the dews of morning by the rising of some Sun of power. Alexander's invincibles are suddenly dissipated into nothingness, as counter winds of heaven neutralize each other into a dead calm. And the triumphant march of the Prussian Emperor, William, to Paris, was the march of a God in History.

Battlefields are the potential results, not of human prowess, but of divine arbitration. Such were Marathon, Zama, Pharsalia, the Invincible Armada, Moscow, Waterloo, Cressy, Agincourt, Lexington, Bunker-hill, Saratoga, Yorktown, New Orleans, Buena Vista, Pittsburgh Landing, and Seven Pines.

History is not a narrative without a moral power. It is not a strange storehouse of Romance, though often stranger than Romance. It is a train of consecutive events with two causes, man and a power above him. It is rather the history of a divine than a human will. Here are welded the links of human destiny, on a splendid scale. A spirit breathes on destiny, and it lives. It comes loaded with treasures for the heart's meditation as well as for the head's reflection.

> "In the atheist declaring,
>   Fatherless are earth and skies,
> He is doubting not desparing;
>   Who can hinder doubts to rise?
> Surely mightier faith constraineth,
>   To deny the DEITY,
> When eternal order reigneth
>   Than believe his agency."

Come, atheist, into this moral field with us and behold the forests, fruits and flowers of design, which embellish the presence of a DEITY.

1. The stupendous narrative is opened by Sacred History when all else of the world's archives was tradition, and no power of printing press yet recorded and multiplied it in books without end. There was a strange peculiar people living in the tents of Mesopotamia, Israelites by name. They were in process of time found in the land and the palace of a Pharaoh. Then came an escape by the sea and the wilderness, in defiance of deserts and of death. In half a century these wanderers suddenly appear clothed and equipped by a miracle; they are formidable warriors before whom fall the cities of Canaan. Without instruction, and evidently by miracle, they develop a civil code, the first ever known; and social life is invited, by them, to be virtuous, a hitherto unknown impulsion. Triumphant battles were fought in which the conquerors only used rams' horns and dark lanterns. Though captivity followed captivity, yet Israel was a unity. Now they were in the "valleys of Goshen," and now by the "rivers of Babylon". They had warriors, rulers, prophets and leaders for every emergency. Around them were formidable empires and

invincible conquerors; yet distinct and unconquered they lived. In all this, who fought for Israel and made them defiant against every human Goliath? The LORD. What for? To impress a knowledge of DEITY; Israel was to be a monumental people forever; to carry a new covenant to the world; to prepare the race for the incarnation of DEITY. That mission being accomplished, Israel, proud, inconsistent, formal, sinful, tumbled into decay, but not before it became an evident retribution for sin. There must be a GOD whom the Jew has offended; no other hypothesis will account for Jewish derision.

2. History records that on the plains of Persia, twenty four centuries ago, a monarch reigned, who, different from all other monarchs of all time, voluntarily, sent from captivity to freedom a whole nation, namely the Jewish. Without this unaccountable liberality of Cyrus the monarch, a broken link would forever have left in banishment the Jew and the significant temple, around which, later, clustered such essential and momentous developments of theory, thought and action. A GOD had commanded, and Cyrus crouched in obedience.

3. Only once did the world ever, from Britain to India, bow to one conquering nation. Why was

the empire of the Caesars universal? Why did it supplant the authority of Saul and of Solomon? Why did purely political power restrain Jewish intoleration? Why should emigration from Jerusalem be made so easy over all the world besides? Evidently some general plan of a GOD was being consummated; some fulness of time had come; some New Testament Revelation must be at hand. It was all explained in the scenes of Bethlehem and Gethsemane.

4. There must be a cradle, a home and a depository, strong and popular for the birth of Literature. Those conditions were obtained when, at the dispersion from Shinar, there went out the sons of Japheth, to the balmy islands and the rich peninsulas of Greece. Cecrops settled Athens; Lelex founded Sparta, Inacus made other settlements and Corinth arose. Cadmus, the Theban, invented the alphabet, the elements of which are now the woof of all written thoughts. Homer sang, and affixed language firmly to the emotions, and Lycurgus and Solon eliminated and planted it, in systems of civil law. Thus the birth of law, language and song, nearly cotemporary, in this fruitful, commercial strong-hold of the world prepared the way for

civilization and for its light to be gleamed over the world, preparatory to some greater event in anticipation. Human thought and human liberty grew into greatness, side by side. They were the theme of poets, the ideal of artists, the engraved product of sculptors, and they were the abiding spirit on the parchment of the historian.

Why this long life of a feeble peninsula? The people without Revelation or spiritual eyes said it was the favor of Jupiter and the gods. The existence of Greece brought the race onward, lifted it upward, and embalmed thought and invention. Greece was thus evidently commissioned to rise and speak to the infant world. The world has not forgotten the lesson to this day, but now wonders in its maturity at the wisdom and the miracle of this great people concentrated chiefly on a few islands. When they had filled the archives of antiquity with their achievements, had become corrupt in religion and bigoted and boastful in civil affairs, then as mysterious a miracle caused their glory to depart.

It was not because Alexander lived, that Greece was perpetuated, for his final acts tended to its disintegration: it was not because Persia was defeated at Marathon, for that victory brought to the surface internal dissensions for a century; it was not the commercial advantages there clustering, for these remain to-day, and the land is only an embodiment of weakness; but her mission was to assist the entire race, the future as well as the present, enemies as well as friends. Her books were the depositories whence the schools of Literature in all ages would draw nourishment; her writers were the pioneers of the world in recovering order of language from the confusion of Babel; her generals had no object in view save ambition, but a power above them brought strange victory at Marathon and Thermopylæ. The power was in part theirs by loan, and in part wholly external, subjective and objective, *ego* and *non-ego*. They were like a tributary of a larger river, flowing on with momentum and majesty, but finally lost in a larger stream. If no DEITY presided over Greece for centuries, then there was effect without cause, which is impossible. The land of Peninsulas perished; but did all of its store of civilization of a thousand years perish? No, there was prepared for all this mental wealth a home in a fostering nation as inheritor.

5. "There was an ancient city, Troy by name." The cruel Grecian had, by strategy, entered its walls and buried its glory in ashes. But from it escaped Æneas, who embarked despite storms and destruction, and landed upon the balmy banks of the yellow Tiber. Though this origin of Rome was, in its details, the fiction of the poet, yet the preparation of such a people and such a city as the "city of seven hills" was a superhuman event. At any rate it became a nation to concentrate the power and foster the wisdom of the world preparatory to some final development, secondary to some ulterior destiny. Civilization was now incarnate in the Roman citizen. It was not because of the gallant Cæsar, the triumphant Pompey, the eloquent Cicero, or the accomplished Horace; it was not because Carthage, Britain, Gaul and the world bowed down in obedience to her warriors; but it was because Rome was a receptacle of ideas which the world was to inherit in the fulness of time. Then corruption came; false theology sprang up from policy; bigoted intolerance was seconded by the fagot and the rack, and retribution followed. Rome went to political dust; but she accomplished a mission in a vaster economy than belongs to a single

national life; for her influence attached to other nations. Modern Popery is a curse to the world, but heathen Rome was overruled into a blessing.

6. But shall Literature perish in Europe's long night? There was a power far surpassing the fanaticism of man, which rescued it. The Crusades came in 1099; the Hermit preached; the Pope proffered unlimited indulgence; the deluded rabble rushed towards Jerusalem; thousands perished; fanaticism killed them; but the residue passed through the birth-place of letters and carried the classic records of antiquity to their homes. Thought was resurrected; men were spiritually emancipated; schools were founded; Luther lived; the Reformation was born; the Mohammedan Crescent, like a pale moon, staid to rule by night in the East, but in the West, the cross uncovered, and purified from popery, has been making day by its own glory. Its beams roll back, dispelling night, a sun of Righteousness, until mentally, morally, commercially, civilly, the crescent is lost amid the day. Rome has been eyeing the Turk for a millennium; the Turk in turn, full of jealousy, has been watching Rome. Some Power, not human, has commanded the one evil to neutralize the other.

7. What of Western Europe? When men, here and there, like monads on the water, apparently motionless, began to think, they struggled; the struggle leavened the whole lump; the maledictions of the Pope did not hinder the benedictions of some higher throne; first Saxony, then all Germany, Switzerland and finally England protested, and that moment a God vindicated himself. There are times in history when moulding forces, beyond and opposed to human, invisible, potential, full of divinity, overwhelm. The Reformation was such a time. While all the world seemed possessed of devils, Luther appeared possesed almost of divine thought, resolution and action. The world yielded and Luther, or rather God, with whom he co-labored, prevailed.

8. One God has ever been believed in English Theology. Therefore England had a history prepared; she was to be military and commercial mistress of land and sea, for ages; she was to give her impress and missionary life to the globe. Not with foreknowledge, but passively, she submitted to the preparation. At the critical juncture Cardinal Woolsey sought the pontifical chair, at the same time Woolsey's king sought divorce through the Pope.

The former fell, but the latter, strong in his passion, fled popery forever, to woo and wed his paramour. That incident freed England from Rome and at the same time, put that enmity between them, which admits of no compromise. The English king and Woolsey and the pope were only automatons of clay worked by a GOD. The problem of the religion and felicity of every nation moulded by British influence, was involved in the event of the two queens just alluded to. Britain, thus emancipated, crowned with success in war and in peace, goes forth, like the angel of the apocalypse "preaching the everlasting gospel."

9. In America "the Lord reigneth." At first France, Spain, Portugal made wide discoveries and essayed vast settlements. England also came, and by apparent accident, occupied the middle belt of land. The decided advantage was in all respects with the popish settlements.

The tropics, semi-tropics, and regions of the north yielded to them, the Mississippi valley was theirs. To protestantism were the forbidding hills of New England and Virginia. The unequal conflict began at the coast and swept westward. History opened; the scene was shifted; years fled; men were astonished; about the protestant idea as a nucleus, by no human design, the settlements have knit into a Protestant unit, free from thralldom, until America, like Canaan for plenty, like Ophir, for gold, like the gardens of Hesperus for beauty, is the mystery of the world. And human motives and means are utterly inadequate to the explanation; it is in the plan of God.

10. The most populous land of the world, China excepted, and the most fruitful, is India. Its Vedas have for ages praised the supremacy of Vishnu; but its millions are crushed, by caste, in crime. Life there was only evil continually; then, apparently to establish a commercial emporium and protect it, British powder flashed in the faces of the reigning chiefs. A handful of British soldiery subdues the crowded millions of India; British law, stern and invincible, holds the lawless hordes until the missionary comes with a broadside of faith, hope and charity. The shackless of ages fall from the bound spirits of India, and to day civilization is far on its way forced by Christianization.

11. Perry, with his gun-boat, thundered at the door of Japan, forced entrance, and that mighty nation is now inviting us to come again with the

implements of our Christianization. Perry's gunboat was the Simon Boanerges whose sermon opened the way for the mild and tender Johns of the apostleship. That second event was not the will of the Japanese Emperor, nor the expectation of Perry, but a second growth of effect matured by the Ruler of Nations.

12. Is there evidence of a God in Africa? The sons of Ham have been passing through a crucible to bring their posterity to a brighter future. Charles V. authorized ships to steal the African into Slavery, and he lingered, like Israel, in a four hundred years bondage. Awhile he dies amid the warm luxuries of the West Indies, and awhile he toils in servitude among the cane and cotton of the South. But the cup is full; there is a God; He is ready; the cannon booms; the nation tumbles, tosses and groans; and the foot of the nation says to the head "I have no need of thee;" red war revels; but by and by, the smoke rises and the man of Africa has come up to liberty. A God has vindicated the right.

The curtain falls to rise again. Scene second follows hard upon the first; the constitutional amendment stamps the former event as monumental; primers, spellers and readers fall among the freedmen like the manna of heaven. And despite Herbert Spencer, despite Darwin, despite Huxley, despite the infidels, to universal brotherhood a mighty discovery was proclaimed—the man of Africa was a living soul, an immortal, and not a black animal.

Scene third is now forming into history. The emancipated African is going home, loaded down with the spoils of civilization. He is now discipling Africa with books, laws, morals, commercial and mechanical prestige. Liberia, lives; Sierra Leone is the

"Home, home, sweet, sweet home"

of the former slave. The wisdom, justice and mercy of some Omnipotent is in the whole transaction. The same God had made

"Afric's sunny fountains
Roll down their golden sands."

13. China boasts absolute unchangeableness for forty centuries as if no God was above them. But their people's jubilee is near. Though wrapt in self-glory and sufficiency sternly as a lion in his lair, yet a divinity is holding them to the mighty prob-

lems of their destiny. A gun-boat thunders at their walls and civilization forces its blessings down upon them. Look over the Pacific; China's counterpart is the "golden gates" of California. They spread open to the world, by an accident apparently human. Fremont climbs the Nevadas, takes possession just prior to the arrival of a hostile Mexican force, and a God makes it the base of

> "His mysterious ways
> He plants his footsteps in the seas."

China wakes up; shakes off the slumbers of a hundred and twenty generations: God invites her to our shores; man threatens, fears, philosophizes; but, divinely invited, the ships of the orient come for our treasures. Behold them return, the path of the sea is a beaten track, and they carry to the eastern empire all the trophies of our own renewed life. Each homeward bound Chinaman carries potent forces, and is commissioned of a God to evangelize his native land.

14. The human idea is monarchy and oppression; the opposite, civil liberty and free personal sovereignty must emanate from a God. Men diverge, are selfish and hostile, but some force reverses this law and impels a segregation of the masses into

a single unity. Crystal Palaces, Peace jubilees, Expositions, General Councils, and International Conventions are significant convergence. But, better, the nations are becoming more fraternal and of one heart. The man of the law, who lives upon legal bickerings and litigations, having less and less employment, is becoming only a fugitive and a vagabond in the earth. Some Prince of Peace has overturned the tables of those feed attorneys who have so long bought and sold the innocent doves of our race. Court dockets are becoming alarmingly short to those who live thereby. Tribes are uniting; patriarchal forms have combined long since into vast civil organizations, scores of tribes and millions of individuals.

Monarchies die; absolute types of government are superseded by constitutional types; demon force and brute force are dying, and self government is taking life. The absolute yields to the limited form, charters creep in, and then the limited forms rise to the dignity of republics. Violent revolution is less rife: this is the steady growth of civil liberty: it culminates in the Republics of the world. This is the platform to which the nations are coming, the platform of inalienable rights and of civil equality: this is the summit of the world's brotherhood. It is so vast, so all embracing in its comprehension, so far beyond the utmost concentration of human plan or power, that a God is certainly the Guide of the Nations.

15. Men rise almost miraculously from obscurity to greatness, from nothingness to might. Personal resolution is not a sufficient cause though that is an element of success. Many a Kirke White of the noblest resolution has fallen into an early grave. Unless a Higher Power battle for the man of success he is overwhelmed with immediate defeat. We cannot particularize. See the vast array of the great of earth, standing like effect to some general, prime cause, eliminating the effect of destiny itself.

Yonder comes Joseph, and the mighty events of Israel's preservation and introduction into Egypt were made sure; yonder is Moses, and the emancipated millions sweep into Canaan with the law and the covenant; Orpheus lives and poetry is born; Confucius philosphizes, and China leads a wiser life; Socrates moralizes and the whole world is better; Hyppocrates the Physician, becomes a Sanitary Oracle, and plagues and diseases are mastered; Alexander commands, and the world is stirred and goaded into activity; Aristotle and Euclid meditate, and Logic and Mathematics take form like fountains from a high void and roll an intellectual stream down the years; the Cæsars reign, and all people harmonize into an empire to receive the CHRIST: Herodotus, Pliny, Tacitus, Plutarch, and Josephus stand forth from the common multitude like the promontories of their native lands, and the voice of Ancient History becomes the voice of GOD; Tertullian, Origin, and Cyprian stand up in the Apostolic Church, and they are sent down to us with the ethical interpretations of the age: Charlemagne comes to the surface, and the Western Empire rises auspiciously with him; Alfred assumes the crown, and Britain is allured away from barbarism; Gengis Khan conquers, and all Asia is instructed in the Arts of government; Wickliffe thunders with truth, and the papacy feels the first shock of a GOD; Chaucer dips his pen in the fire of thought, and the English Language in its infancy, is baptized with literary light; Columbus pleads with and persuades kings and queens, and America is added to creation; Copernicus considers the heavens, and Astromomy is henceforth beautifully clothed with truth; Raphael and Michael Angelo cast colors on the canvas, and Æsthetics is added to the pleasure of mortals; Luther, Calvin, Knox, and Wesley emerged from the great, bad host of darkness, and infidelity and moral wrong, wounded, slowly retreat home to perdition; blind Milton dipped his pen into the foam of Pierus, and the songs of men float up among the songs of angels; Newton, in the falling apple had a new revelation from heaven, it was true Philosophy; Pitt incarnated the sweet spirit of Liberty; Franklin had the "good and perfect gift" of electricity, in the flash of lightning from the "Father of light;" Washington fought and prayed, and a divinity comes down in the battles for America; Buonaparte rose, conquered and fell at the critical time to leave the infant America unmolested and yet to keep our enemies engaged; Wilberforce breathed benevolent emotions and benedictions, and the bonds of slavery were severed; Marshall of the Judiciary and Clay of Congress held up the nation in auspicious growth. Finally from the snow-capped Kearsarge, comes to life the man who, solid as the granite of his native state, eloquent as the GOD-speaking hills and landscapes where his childhood expanded, loyal to the Union and the nation as the

White Mountains to the rock-ribbed earth, holds the nation entranced by his solidity, eloquence and loyalty while he lived; but when Webster died secession revived. All these men were workmen of a Grand Designer. Their achievements were more than heroic: they were prompted, moved, directed and inspired by a Supreme Governor.

16. The human hand has been educated as well as the head and heart. It is difficult to estimate the power of the hand. Yet it is only a lump of clay, unless it be guided. Some formulas, for its laws, must be known. Some discoveries and inventions must rise up to set the millions of hands to work. Are inventors the creatures who pick up what they stumble upon? Did the heroes of invention, self-taught, unaided, push forward to accomplish work of creation from nothing, or is there not the sign of a God superintending and aiding at the appropriate juncture? Manifestly the latter.

Not accident, but a Revelation of Science, discovered the use of magnifying glasses and opened the way for the Microscope which looks beneath us, and the Telescope which looks above us. Not accident developed the cable and the electric current which embrace and shock the world. Not accident sent medical discovery to the appropriate alleviation of disease. Not accident found the Lode-stone and made the Compass to guide thousands over the deep. Not atheism nor accident made paper and the art of writing. Not infidelity nor human genius inducted the world into printing. The skill of Worcester, Savery, Newcomen, Watts and Fulton in perfecting steam power was the reflection of the skill of a universal GOD. No one of these men ever could have designed or comprehended, and less could have executed a fraction of the results of his invention. A co-operative spirit worked with them: it was GOD.

17. From all these inventions by inexplicable design spring up the trade and commerce of the world. Hidden islands and continents rise up before the compass-guided, steam-driven ships. Lands of beauty and of riches enter the field of discovery, until everywhere the bound of civilization is increased in the ever rolling, ever restless voyages of ships. The abounding wealth of the east comes to bless the west, and the bread of the west crosses oceans to feed the hungry east. The tropical south is bound to the frigid north by a law of reciprocal dependence, indicating the same Providence reign-

ing amid the snows of the pole and the fruitful beams of a zenith sun.

> " This is Thy work, Almighty Providence!
> Whose power, beyond the reach of human thought,
> Revolves the orbs of Empire, bids them sink,
> Deep in the dead'ning night of thy displeasure,
> Or rise majestic o'er a wondering world."

18. These grand results of commerce divide the work of the world into many co-ordinate parts. Division of labor urges its highest perfection : industry has its strongest impulse ; and the race becomes a universal brotherhood, a mutual aid society to expel want and inaugurate luxury for the lap of all people. The anti-tariff man invites free exchange all over the world; and GOD's general legislation is unmistakably upon the same liberal basis. Thus England, full of people is invited of GOD to congregate in cities and become the universal center of manufacturing. America is invited by fruitful soil and timely rain to spread her acres with golden grain. Maritime and river regions seek the wave, the swimming multitudes and finny monsters. The arctic dweller shivers in the fur of the fallen beast: and each man finds his destiny fixed by invisible power. Thus nations are the counterpart of na-

tions; empires are socially and commercially the reciprocal fractions of other empires; continents are bound to continents by more than the speaking cable or the rocky masonry of earth: they are bound by common interest and fraternal love. Wars and disintegration are from the Spirits of darkness, stirring the lusts of the race; but when a voice proclaims by such indissoluble bonds, the highest authority for a life of undisturbed unity in all the world,

"It 's
A divinity that shapes our ends,
Rough hew them how they will."

19. Yonder in Armenia is a little group, the first family of earth; it has no competitor in title to the lands and resources running to waste and decay for want of masters. There were not owners enough to heap up and preserve the abundance of nature. But when the family was increased to millions, alienated in hostility, and all resources were appropriated in fee simple, then who shall decide titles, protect weakness, dispense justice, legislate righteousness, build up empire and establish boundaries to the exclusion of strife, the compacting of every man into a nation, and every nation into a common brotherhood? Who attempting to solve the

grave difficulty, shall prevent the revolution of extermination? Who shall calm and control such a mighty momentum of will-power from heated strife to such perfect harmony that one frail Queen shall sway in peace two hundred millions, and one frail President shall administer laws to forty millions? Such power is not earthly, visible, limited, it is above us, omniscient, omnipresent, omnipotent, it is the mighty GOD.

20. Mind is fed at the table of a GOD. Not all treasures administer to the carnal. How many millions of gold, in its resurrection from earth, assumes the spiritual and mental! Now it takes the form of millions of primary school buildings: now it rises in the brick and mortar of the University or College, full of cabinets, apparatus, libraries, and appliances of wonder: now these golden resources, take equivalent in the mental result, moving in well-wrought intelligence, endowing mind and securing to youthful millions that symmetrical development which ornaments the highest civilization. Why all this expense and sacrifice? GOD has an object to encourage. Talent uninspired of its GOD is asleep, stupid, inactive, nay, dead. Indolence is the unspoken watch-word of man the animal, it is written

on his limbs his bones, his brain: indolence is the grave digger of a soul sojourning in a body which only "lives to eat": but something calls the mind, wakes it and breathes in a full breath of immortal thought. See now its burning emotions: behold it rise, in grandeur, to maintain its sublime flights for a generation, gathering mental treasures from all the universe!

21. History, like a perpetual oracle, demonstrates, that man has a Helper, a Co-worker, a Senior Partner, may we reverently say? a Spirit that leads him on to victory and power in the fields he never trod before. Who is that Co-worker? A God.

> "I asked myself what this great God might be
> That fashioned me?
> I answered: The all-potent, solely immense,
> Surpassing sense;
> Unspeakable, inscrutable, eternal—
> Lord over all.
> The only terrible, strong, just and true,
> Who hath no end and no beginning knew."

"The Lord reigneth" in the nations! The authority for such conclusion is overwhelming. A God superintends, nay, makes the history of the world in all ages. A hand holding all hands, is leading; a Spirit inspiring all spirits, is guiding; a plan surmounting all plan, is moulding in all the vast uncertainties of the world. Blind is the eye that sees it not; obdurate is the heart that feels it not; wild and mad is the monstrosity that denies it. God mounts the throne of history. He metes out destiny to the race; He is an all-absorbing, all-prevailing, all-overwhelming certainty in the convictions of a thoughtful, impartial witness. To assure that conviction, go, read the profound transactions of God as written in all history. Let the mountain of evidence accumulate in the testimonies of Herodotus, Livy, Thucydides, Polybius, Sallust, Strabo, the wretched Hume, and Gibbon, Prescott, Macaulay, Bancroft, Guizot, Goodrich, Wilson, and ten thousand historical secretaries who are the busy amanuenses of a living God. To this add all the unwritten experience and observation of every candid inhabitant of the globe, and the potent and inevitable truth comes pouring in from all the ages, and from all the witnesses of the world, "*There is a* GOD OF HISTORY."

CHAPTER III.

The God of Moral Government.

THERE was a date in eternity past when nothing existed but a God on his throne, and space and duration. No angel had yet been created, no life. The stars did not exist, but a broad, deep, illimitable, dark ocean of chaos, struck its waves hard upon the throne of God. We anticipate the Creation, in this part of the argument, the better to finally derive the *a posteriori* certainty.

The sublime account is rescued from the same chaos by the only witness, the Spirit. That Spirit writes. The awfully sublime words are still more striking, if taken fresh from the Hebrew: "*Berosheth bara Elohim eth hashshamayim veeth haarets*" &c.:—"In beginning created God to wit, the heavens, and to wit, the earth. And the earth became desolation and emptiness, and darkness on face of deep and Spirit of God brooding on face of Waters. And said God, '*become light*,' and became light."

Light, insufferable splendor, is the robe of the divine Majesty we seek. Space was, but it was desolation and emptiness. There was first a brooding then a command, then elements came and atoms existed. The mighty mass of raw material rushed and huddled, like a chaos, impatiently waiting the next command. It was Chaos, the solemn, black shroud wrapping the Universe, formless chaos, deep, massive, impenetrable chaos, chaos unmixed, until the divine brightness speak.

But lo! a movement; beams of a divinity peer in the gloom; the equipage and livery of heaven are astir; the chariot of power rides forth; there is movement on the deep; there is a momentous stir as if universal uncertainty were agitating; it must be the Spirit of a God brooding upon the face of the waters. Had there been angels then, how impressive that awful silence! The eternal sleep of chaos is ended. Behold a voice gives forth this first command, this business mandate of might: "*Let there be light.*" Luminous atoms leap forth from the loaded chariot of God, and shoot the blaze of day into the deep, dark, skyless void. The massive darkness, like a retreating, baffled host, slowly pulled its shadows backward. A Jehovah must have forced its rapid route by dividing the light from the darkness. Day was born: chaos died: and GOD's voice pushes the victory. The second day dawns. The firmament like a tented pavilion rises: the waters stand back: physical day is inaugurated. Eternity is the solemn clock of GOD, while days, months, years, are given as the time-pieces of men. Thus we have a glimpse of the Bible record for fact, and now revert to the harmony of *Moral Government* with *Mosaic Record.*

GOD's plan is a gradual disclosure of his moral law. He is sending every day additional light to the world in the form of rewards and punishments. Man beholds the mighty exhibition of GOD, and applauds or hisses, laughs or weeps, or in darkness wraps his soul forever from the scene. But in it all the evidence of Deity is overwhelming. Wilkins says: "Physical and mathematical certainty may be styled infallible, and moral certainty may be properly styled indubitable."

From natural to moral Creation we follow the divine guidance. The voice which made natural light for the physical globe, ended the creative tumult in rest. But the sleepless Spirit began brooding over the moral deep. The glory beams of a moral government must be flung across the ages. We now see not only that "The heavens declare the glory of God," not only that "The Lord reigneth," but that "He rules in righteousness." We may clearly behold the world's actions followed by rewards and punishments This impartial, but inevitable sequence is so certain that we must accept it as the constant proof of a God. Let us institute the search.

"Let us together beat this ample field,
Try what the open, what the covert yield:
Laugh where we must, be candid where we can,
But always vindicate the ways of God to man."

1. *Moral fitness in the dominion of earth.* The lion is a noble animal, larger, stronger, more enduring than man. The eagle is strong and bold, and disdains to stay on earth, but scorns it from above. The whale, leviathan of the great deep, is prodigious in size, and dangerous, dashing, daring in power. But was any of these to have dominion on earth? No: but rather, a *weak body*, without the shaggy mane and hairy fleece of the lion, without the feathery equipage and hostile talons of the eagle, with-

out the massive momentum or impenetrable skin of the leviathan, was chosen for him who should have dominion. Were it the lion, he would say "It is by my might," were it the whale, he would say "It is by my strength," were it the eagle, he would have tried in rebellion to rise to the throne of the Most High, but in the weak, unprotected, limited body of man was placed dominion with the "breath of lives." Dominion came, not to stocks and stones, not to lion, whale nor eagle, but relatively to the weakest body of the world, that the mighty should be confounded. Here is moral compensation: this first lesson of moral government is reflexive, the lesson of *humility*. Pride was in the eagle, sulky disdain in the lion, and confiding egotism in the whale, but in man, the most defenseless, was expected the grace of humility. The image of GOD was not in body, for he "has not form of parts like a man," but it was in soul and mind, and by these he should have dominion. "He that ruleth his own spirit is better than he that taketh a city." Thus humility in the dominion of self was the first and brightest emanation of moral government.

2. *Moral government allied to human creation.* Erroneous conjectures of human origin would rule out

revelation, and accept tradition and the vile isms of infidelity. Curiosity asks: Did these body spirits grow from the swarm of the limpid marsh? did some angel try his creative skill upon our bodies? or did an inferior divinity of polytheism make us while his neighbor demi-god made our antipodes? did man mediately grow amid the plants of Eden, and accidentally absorb spiritual fire and live? None of these. The mystery of human origin was a secret in heaven for twenty-five centuries: then came the solution. It was a corroboration of moral government, on tables of stone, which the meekest man got from heaven. The question was settled: "GOD made man in his own image," "Hail holy light!" candle of the LORD, shining in the past up to the fountain of human existence, full of the proclamations of a Moral Governor. GOD must be the Author of such existence and such Revelation of it.

3. *The moral laws and the natural which discover immortality to man presuppose and prove a God.* Does each life end in a tragedy of death? We live; but what means this dissolution? do Abel and those who follow him to dust, turn wholly to dust eternal? Does the "breath of life" lose itself in the breeze, and become common air? A flower start-

ed up in April, in May it bloomed, and the world admired, in June it faded and fell, and in July it was dissipated into specks of the flying winds. A butterfly fluttered down on the first genial sunbeam of spring: it was beautiful as the rain-bow of God, and numerous bevies of children chased it to admire, but as one touched it, it fell, it fluttered to pieces, it was made of colored earth, the wind swept the place where it fell and it was gone forever. A colt was in the meadow; he tenderly nipped the timothy, soon he waxed fat and kicked as Jeshuran. In a decade of years he pranced in his power and tossed his mane in pride; but at twenty he tumbled to dust; even his bones enriched the soil, and the daring, giant steed was a part of the alluvial mass. Is it so with man? The babe of yesterday is the youth of to day, the man of tomorrow, and the next day his body lends curvature to the mound of the valley. His dust dies; reason reels; and darkness divides this life from futurity; but a voice above, that administers moral government, proclaims above the din of death: "Let the light break on man's destiny:" let there be ceaseless duration for rewards and punishments. No wonder this quenchless desire, this "lamp of immortality," burns up, like a lighthouse, where the breakers strike around the rocks of death, and then I hear the voice of some God-Spirit say: "If a man die he *shall* live again." This lamp casts the blaze of day forward as well as backward to the very dawn of eternal day. I recognize that solemn voice of authority as a GOD.

4. *The light of moral government must explode Polytheism forever.* The man who talked "face to face" with GOD, on the mountain, was unborn; the tables of stone were prospectively dashed in pieces, and their thrilling tradition was an idle tale. Human life, with nine hundred years before it, was at liberty to theorize. The old tradition of creation was forgotten; giants grew—giants in infidelity, in atheism, in forgetfulness, in wickedness. The world must learn the lesson of one GOD; it would not. But a moral government, clothed with the tragedy, the awful lessons of the flood, rolled that stubborn world into the flood and the experiment of man receded more than sixteen centuries, and creation began anew as a reward to righteous Noah and a punishment to all else. The lesson of that retribution was "There is one GOD." But man forgot the lesson; that scene went to oblivion;

man multiplied; sin multiplied; moral darkness multiplied; atheism multiplied; free-thinking multiplied; isms multiplied. To some, the generative power of Jupiter was supreme. Others venerated the ideal Saturn, the time god; others most feared the conscience-scourging, crime-avenging Furies; others paid supreme worship to the rosy, charming, myrtle-loving Venus; others most feared the earth-shaking Neptune; others paid homage to Pluto, the deaf, sulphur god; others dwelt in tragedy and blood and bowed to Mars; others, inebriated in the fiery drafts of wine, adored only Bacchus; others made holiday to Isis and Osiris; others built high places to the glory of Baal. The seaman had his god, the landsman his, the husbandman his, the vine dresser his, the shepherd his, the warrior his. O the Chaos! the formless, void wild! the wicked inventions from the heartless head! the cheerless, rainless, rayless moral drought! O for a shower of light to show us who is God! O for an exhibition of moral government that will burn truth, testimony and faith into human hearts! Then Moses hears a voice of awful authority, of jealous dignity, with one proclamation excluding all pretenders and rivals: "Thou shalt have no other gods before me."

Earth becomes dumb; these gods are dumb idols. The same Jehovah multiplies miracles then to assure the faith of man and illuminate his reason. Defiant of Jupiter, Neptune, Pluto and the whole retinue, he sweeps the antédiluvian world into the death shadows. He breaks the infidelity of Egypt and Israel with matchless, awful plagues, and confirms the lesson of a divinity by the sea-burial of a GOD-defying Pharaoh. He stands on Sinai and raises the glory of his power in a Decalogue. He confounds the Canaanite by turning to destruction a walled city. He converts three kings and nations simply by "stopping the mouths of lions, and quenching the violence of fire." The lesson to the nations was one of the existence, energy and disposition of GOD. He beats back the chaos of error, and proclaims the light of truth in these miracles more emphatically than when light was created.

5. *God's moral government is not always immediate.* The deliberations of GOD involve ages. Having all eternity at command, GOD can make his natural and moral laws gradual, deliberate and adapted to the slow comprehension of finite minds. The earth's crust was not hurried through by the Master Builder. He was hoarding up in it rewards for the fu-

ture man. Ages were his own. And as the woodman counts the age of a tree by the rings of its growth, so God keeps the records of earth's age for us to read in its strata. This progressive method of God was illustrated by the first day's twilight and the later appointment of sun and moon: then by the gradual unfolding of the divine nature and moral plans: and then in the exaltation of the redeemed from earth's darkness to the "far more exceeding and eternal weight of glory." So visions of His moral government, to day, would be too dazzling in degree for Methuselah, Job, or Jonah. The way opens to science and religion, but at that time man's spiritual eyes were only adapted to twilight. Noon would be to him a sunstroke or a blindness. Instead of the hurry of miracles, was the slow, but impressive activity of moral laws. Mind was left, nay, invited to plod onward in discovery. The highest pleasure to pure mind is to "seek and find," to "knock and have it opened," to dig deep, soar high, bring from afar, to glory in the acquisition, to exult in originality. This is man's reward; diligence is rewarded with a sweet daily feast of pleasure. In harmony with this inner law of pleasure, some God has left scientific truth, unrevealed, for the mind. Truth is in envelopes. Who will, may remove the cover and have the truth. The fruit of mind has but to be stripped of its pericarp and the rich kernel is ours. There are rewards to the devout reader, the profound thinker, the intense observer. Human mind must have a Heavenly Father that pets it with the sweet-meats of pleasure. The eye looks up. Above, the blue sea of glass rises overhead and rests all around the horizon on the margin of the distant land. The first careless view regarded it as a solid crystal, turned over the flat, habitable earth, having windows through which rain poured and angels passed. This was called firmament, the solid, transparent, crystalline sphere. Yet man, unsatisfied, gazed and slowly the light revealed that this was not a solid firmament, but the clear, blue sky all the way up to heaven; it was the glorious outside of heaven, whose inside is the gorgeous home of the soul; and it will be sweet reward to see the within.

Adam was not created on a high mountain, for his body, seeking to learn the law of gravitation, might fall into destruction. To know that law required ten years of profound thought, then moral government brought such an overwhelming reward to Newton, whose years of patience undertook the problem, that pleasurable consciousness lapsed into stillness and powerlessness in the awful Presence, while an assistant completed the figures. The first Astronomer beheld the sun rising from deep space in the morning, culminating at noon, then declining to the dark abyss of evening and diving into hidden deep space, until morning again. He thought earth fixed, central and royal with the sun as only our revolving lamp. Hence says Joshua "Sun, stand thou still upon Gibeon and Moon, in the valley of Ajalon." But later, moral government has rewarded with inestimable pleasure, the devout Astronomer, who has eliminated the theory of the Copernican system.

6. *Conscience bears witness to moral government.* The will of God could be known before Revelation was known, otherwise millions must wither in chaos. But conscience ever interposes, dictating with the force of divine law. Conscience within reflected its Maker and the righteousness of His law. It recognized right and wrong, reward and penalty; happiness and misery. Invisible design coupled all effects righteously with causes and the fool was confounded who said in his heart "There is no

God." Conscience was the assistant of Nature in Theology. Everywhere people were forced to say "How terrible is this place." "God is in this place." They saw Him in the deep thunder, for it often struck down wickedness; He was in the red lightnings, for they sometimes brought sudden destruction; He was in the heavy volcano, for proud cities were often covered with lava; He was in the rending earthquake, for impenitent people were sunk in its chasms; He was in the roaring sea and the stormy sky, for the faithless Peters must sink and the disobedient Jonahs must go overboard; He was in the blooming spring, the leafy summer, the fruited autumn and the congealing winter, for they brought plenteous stores to the industrious, and starvation to the indolent.

7. *That rewards and punishments follow the proper use or abuse of our bodies, implies a God of moral government.* Every rational creature, though a heathen, must ejaculate "I am fearfully and wonderfully made." Neither Jupiter with his thunderbolts, Neptune with his trident, nor Pluto with his bident could bring health for temperance, or disease for exposure. This was God. Here are bones framed and fitted with balls and sockets,

tenon and mortise, firmness and elasticity, cartilage and ligament, curvature and adaptation. Here are muscles with expansion and contraction, power and rapidity, delicacy and deliberation, wonder and symmetry. Here are nerves with sensation and feeling, motion and communication, infinitely multiplied branches, and both special and general uses. Here are heart and capillaries, arteries and veins, open channels and crimson currents. Here are organs and systems and works of wonder and universal harmony. To all these proclaims a moral Governor "Thou shalt not abuse this body." Men refuse to obey and anon come the penalties. Ague, apoplexy, cramps, dyspepsia, fevers, neuralgia, smallpox, cholera, death. Even in the body, right ever has a reward, and wrong a punishment. Tradition, observation, experience, history all agree in proof of this invariable portion to all. Retributive law is in it. Whoever dines on too much luxury is punished with dyspepsia; he who drinks firey wine, becomes a raving, frothing idiot; he who sleeps day away has stupor in his head and weeds in his garden; he who turns night into day, breathing its limpid air, generates neuralgia or catarrh in the air passages and may find a grave with consumptives; he who abuses the body with too much pressure will reap corns and cancers, short breath and deformity, bruises and putrefying sores; he who swings his neck from a rope or rashly rushes into deep water, or takes poison, or leaps from a precipice, will invariably die in disgrace; and he who uses tobacco must become filthy; but he, who by temperance in all things and obedience to evident law, seeks the good, is blessed with long life, health and happiness.

He who detests the drudgery of strong, original thought, is puny and senseless; he who avoids schools, books and observation, is ignorant and silly; but he who sternly measures the deep channels of thought, and makes all men, objects and relations his teachers, will be rewarded with culture, credit and satisfaction. He who cultivates the good will of neighbors and friends will never lack close friends; but he who, by base selfishness and indifference, spurns the tender feelings of friendship, must become a fugitive and a vagabond from society. Whoever seeks the true and right, as guides to duty, will be eminent for integrity and will achieve the rewards of self government and virtue.

The city which bands to do wickedly is soon inherited by owls and bats, or smoking and sinking amid storms of falling fire, or biting ashes; while the city that inscribes justice and righteousness on its gates, exceedingly prospers. The state, nation or tribe, which dared to obey these clear laws of sequence, towered in the glory of its nationality, while the people that cultivated iniquity and ruled by oppression, speedily fell by some invisible stroke. Thus fell Sodom and Gomorrah, Egypt and the Canaanites, then at last Israel and Judah, Nineveh and Babylon, Assyria and Moab, Ethiopia and Tyre, Persia and Macedon, Carthage and Troy, Chaldea and Edom. The works and rewards of these were illustrative of the solemn record. Man saw it and said "Whosoever doeth these things is a Ruler in Righteousness" and of universal dominion.

8. *This proof of a God seen in his moral government is strengthened by the final object of moral government.* All intelligences are admonished of wrong and pointed to right. They are warned of the final disposition of a God to both the good and the evil. They behold life a trial. While it is probation to the creature it infolds the existence and

will of the Creator. It is to test endurance; defects may be corrected; weakness may be strengthened and infirmity may be amended. Probation is the opportunity; men are on probation; angels were perhaps once on probation; cities and states are on probation; earth itself is running its probation with the family of man; and spirit, not matter is tried. Gravity holds us to the probation of earth; we cannot rise above it. In childhood we watch the beautiful, white clouds as they float onward like free spirits of the sky in golden palaces or on mountains of variegated glory, and we desire to become voyagers in fancy on these free dissolving clouds. But up there is the region of the DEITY. He says to man, "Stay beneath on trial a little time; seek moral heights, not dissolving clouds; get on heavenly highways; let earth recede from the heart; wait until the chariot of DEITY come to bid us higher." Elisha may gaze wishfully after Elijah who mounts the chariot of fire, but the spirit bids Elisha catch the falling mantle, go back, wait and work a little longer.

A parent holds out the bright watch of gold to the tottering year old babe, as an inducement to walk to theparental knee; so some Father of the Soul, holds out the stars of night, as watches from the pocket of heaven, to urge the tottering faith, "to run and not weary, walk and not faint." Moral government leads the soul up to its home, and by the satisfaction of reward "the path of the just shineth brighter and brighter to the perfect day;" behind it recedes the "outer darkness" for the spirits of darkness, a retreat for devils. This earth is a *camera obscura* to better develop the landscapes of light. In the mixed good and evil is design which vindicates a divine Author. These attractions are to draw all men up and reward them for coming: these dark repulsions are to drive, urge, warn, deter men from the chaos of perdition, and punish their tendencies thither. The provider of so wise a plan is a GOD.

9. *God discloses himself in the moral probation which rewards the good with himself as a co-worker, and punishes the evil by leaving them alone.* So freely are men invited to co-labor with the DEITY, that many a man, nay, whole empires and continents have done it, while others have abused the freedom and power, expelling the heavenly Partner by their wickedness. In this high partnership the infinite

wisdom of the Senior Partner becomes a blessed reward of the junior probationer. This God is a teacher, while man is a learner. Man has not instinct to lend accuracy to his inferences, while God stoops amid the turbulence and discord. God does not neglect us to make distant worlds, nor to govern his central heaven. Nor does he only come occasionally as a circuit judge to hold a court of appellate jurisdiction, when men fail to agree, or of equity when the stronger, in unequal strife, force the weaker to appeal; nor does he leave to men the control of things trivial and individual, while himself only appears in cases of magnitude, such as the government of cities, states, empires, armies, and in commercial and general interests. This Moral Governor, co-working with man, does not pamper him in simpering idleness; man is not to be still, as if incapable of any action; he may not rest his weak arm in inactivity, to be worked by the Strong Arm; man may not repudiate thought, hoping for thought by spontaneous creation; but rather, rich rewards fall upon him who thinks, plans, works, legislates, decides, executes in his proper sphere. Above man is an evident power, now helping in right, now hindering in wrong, now like a presiding officer reserving the casting vote, when men are balanced in disagreement, now using a veto, when human actions oppose divine wisdom, and now repeal and abolishment, when finite schemes are obnoxious to the Infinite. There is certainly a Superintending Wisdom in these tender rewards and gentle punishments which may become exceeding and eternal with the action of man. Of course ignorant man is justly excluded from any legislation in this general government of the Universe, though some men feel slighted when not consulted on these affairs of the universe. In the establishment of general laws, GOD excludes wholly the chance for failure, as for instance the transportation of his subjects from this world by death, in the change which comes in the "twinkling of an eye." Neither man's aid nor his option may arouse departed Spirits. The theory that spirits of heaven or hell communicate with men on earth is contrary to moral government. As, if man were not content to co-work with DEITY on earth, he must go with proud Lucifer, Son of the morning, and wake up heaven and hell by tapping on a table, or fooling with a planchette. All theories of Spiritualism are opposed to moral government. Are spirits loose from their prisons, insubordinate to the Great Ruler and skulking under chairs and tables? Charon, who ferries spirits over the river of death, by the fabled allusion, never carries a return load in his boat. Spirits may not intrude among men; men may not go among spirits and return again. The Eternal Spirit, who governs all, must be everywhere with his right hand of blessedness and his left hand of banishment. In his rounds He sets opposite this nation the star, with the foot-note "passed away," opposite that city, "overturned and razed," opposite this man's name, "died in the faith," opposite that name, "lost."

There is a God. His moral government is a light to the nations; it comes to man in the potent rays of Revelation; it shines from Sinai, from the Power-God, the Justice-God; it beams in the clear, evident disclosures to man of his origin by creative word, and his final doom by the words of judgment; it pours floods of light to discover man's immortality; it burns to the annihilation of the gods of polytheism; it reveals the slow roll of an eternity in the plan; it shines upon the rewards of the righteous, as a pillar of fire, and, as a pillar of cloud, it hides from the wicked all hope in his wickedness; it gleams upon the design of man's probation, until the spirit takes in the present and the future as one piece of existence; and it finally reveals the hand of the good man in the hand of GOD, as a co-worker.

The earth itself rushes on to its destruction; but beyond the firmament, beyond the sky of blue and the clouds of black, high above the sweeping surges of change, there must be unchangeableness; there must be a GOD; there must be happiness; there must be eternal day. This moral government promises and demands it, and the soul longs, and muses and plumes for the immortal flight. Light breaks; it is burnished from the grand center of day; it pours down from the mountains of glory; up that mountain hies the spirit of man until he finds at its crown the Fountain Spring of moral light, and behold, it is a GOD.

CHAPTER IV.

The God of the Bible.

HAMLET had his Shakspeare; Paradise Lost its Milton; the Pilgrim's Progress its Bunyan; the Human Understanding its Locke; the Spectator its Addison; the Deserted Village its Goldsmith; Childe Harold its Byron; Marmion its Walter Scott; Pickwick its Dickens; the Iliad its Homer; the Madonna its Raphael; the Pyramid its Architect, and *the Bible has its God.*

Man staggers under great enterprises, he faints and utterly dies, if he attempts the supernatural, and, in the achievements demanding centuries, he is arrested by time and hurried off to eternity long before his schemes are matured. This Bible is wonderful, supernatural, the work of centuries, evidently divine. A book, as such, must be written during the life of its author. It may undergo revision; others may analyze; friend or foe may derive a synopsis. Introductions, prefaces, addendas and appendices by others may encumber the future edition, but the body of the work is the same. Books are generally composed in a few months. No man dare spend a half century upon his work; so changeable are sentiment and taste that the fiftieth year would only be a denial of the first year's assertions. But the Bible, with steady plan and a harmony of parts, lingered in its formation fifteen and a half centuries, from the man Moses, before his mountain burial on Nebo, to John on Patmos, penning the last words of the "Alpha and Omega of all things." The author of the Bible must have lived all these centuries, and must have been unchangeable also. Man's longest life of an hundred and twenty years is at least thirteen times too short to have given the Bible existence. Therefore some unchangeable, eternal God must have written it.

1. *Human testimony traces the Bible to its Author, God.* No book ever grew, or crystalized, or fell by accident into shape. Each thought had birth in mind before its existence on parchment; even anonymous books have authors, though they be un-

known. We may institute an inquiry; seek the printer; from the printer we go to the proof reader; thence we hasten to the editor and publisher; here the manuscript with all its interlinears, erasures, additions and subtractions, is before us; it is now but one step back to the study of the author. Here are his pens, his ink-fountain, his paper, his table, his chair, and in it is the identical hero of the book, the Author.

The Bible is such a book, a fact. Whose mind dictated it? whose thought lives in it? let us together walk to its cradle, let us discover its birth. Back we go 270 years to the days of king James I. of England. By his appointment forty-seven men, the best scholars of the Classics in all the realm, translated the Bible from its original. Except by dust-dealing infidels, the result was universally confessed to be a true and faithful rendering of the manuscript. Whence came that manuscript into a unity? 569 manuscripts in Greek, of the New Testament, and 751 in Hebrew of the Old Testament were found. Some of these were partial, none entire, but many covering each special book of the Bible. These came down on parchment rolls, papyrus flag, or tables of wood or stone.

Hundreds of witnesses, defying the ages, thus solemnly held the oracles. But let us follow back this harmonious flood of manuscript. We trace it sixteen, seventeen and eighteen centuries, when clouds of witnesses arise to testify the united opinion of the Church. Fresh from the death bed of the Apostles, the whole Church assembled in councils and prayerfully and carefully pronounced inspired and authorized the present books of the Bible. These books were as well known and as readily received then as now, by the spreading Church in all Western Asia, Northern Africa and Europe. Catalogues of them were printed, Commentaries were written, a distinct volume was made on which was inscribed "Holy." Quotations were derived, public readings were instituted, and all Christian Churches, just after the apostolic days, when the volume was finished, accepted, adopted and sacredly used it without hesitation. From this mighty array came thousands of manuscripts, of which hundreds as aforesaid, reached our translators. Thus we have reached the fountain of the New Testament.

In such origin the Fathers confirm the testimony of Paul, Peter, John, Mark, Matthew and Luke, that they were the writers of the books ascribed to them. Thus the Church from the first to the fourth century, testifies to the genuineness, authenticity and credibility of the books; thus they express a confidence so deep in these writers that they rest eternal salvation upon their message. But what did the profane, unbelieving world do? The same as now; they accepted the Bible as a stubborn fact, but caviled at its plans and provisions with evasive excuses and faults. Thus the New Testament comes down from the Gross, the Manger, the Transfiguration and the Ascension

The Old Testament is of higher antiquity, but it has a jealous Jewish nation of millions, keeping sacred its oracles. Each of the millions would be a swift, loud witness against one jot or tittle of corruption in the sacred text. The standard copy was kept, in the days of the Temple, in the Holy of Holies, where no vandal pen could add or erase a particle. By most careful appointment, as if their soul's destiny depended upon it, they inaugurated a chief Scribe, who should keep and add the truly divine to the record, as God gave it to man. When it consisted of the five books of Moses only, it came through the wilderness from Sinai, where it first took form from the mouth of GOD as Moses made the preservation. It was in the Ark of the Covenant with the Pot of Manna and the Flowering Rod, and above it was the visible illumination of the Shekinah. When Solomon built the new Temple which GOD filled, in that Temple was placed most sacredly in trust, the same precious Mosaic record, to which had been added Joshua, Judges, the Psalms, and much of Solomon's inspired writings. Here rested the forming Bible until the Temple was destroyed by Nebuchadnezzar, but duplicates had already gone out into every land, and parchments like the Bible of to-day, had reached every Jewish home. Nothing but a miracle, such as destroyed the first-born in Egypt, could have taken from earth and recalled to heaven all the copies of the Bible. Hence when the Temple was destroyed the Bible lived on, immortal as its GOD, and GOD lived on immortal as his own words of truth. At the restoration from Babylon by Cyrus, Ezra and the Great Synagogue, of whom Malachi, the prophet, was the last, carefully added the prophecies in the captivity, and the final words of Malachi, and placed them in the Temple rebuilt. This double precaution was taken when the pure and true copies could have been obtained all over Israel and wherever a Jew had wandered. That this outline is true and credible, is made certain by profane as well as sacred writers, by enemies as well as friends, by cotemporaries as well as immediate posterity.

Thus we have gone back to the burning, smoking mountain of Sinai, and behold the Old Testament comes from a voice of authority above the mountain, in clouds of fire and flashes of flaming sky. And, as the man Moses, carried down the mountain his revelation of the Divine, his face shone with illumination, and the people saw it and believed, "but Moses wist not that his face shone." Oh! the power of unconscious influence which God gives to a countenance of clay! We have traced the preservation through its additions by prophecy and its multiplications by sacred Scribes, and we have seen how it spread over the wide land, though the Jew go into captivity and Judea be a desolation. Thus it joined the New Testament as *the Book*, sacred, holy, the unity of a divine will. That it was not corrupted, is evident when we reflect that its identity in the smallest orthography and painting was insisted upon with the gravest penalties for mistakes, and the utter repudiation of all for even one error. The value of the book to the Jew depended upon its accuracy. It was impossible to mar it because of the vast number of copies extant and the well known reading to the congregations of the synagogue. Not even the desolation of war and captivity could destroy it, for it was now a hydra-headed manuscript of vast multiplicity. Such changes must have been all guarded against by an author GOD.

2. *The Bible is one, and therefore has but one Author.* The newer portion is replete with quotations from the older; the Apostles make authority of Moses and the prophets. The new quotes the old as inspired. Each Scribe accepts all others, and thus forty writers stand in corroboration and proof of each other. If therefore Matthew send a divine message, so must Isaiah. If Malachi stand the test, he carries the forty writers with him. This granted, it follows that a common mind inspired all to write by dictation. This conclusion brings us by necessity to a GOD who alone could live through the ages. The spirit that pervades all is one spirit. Here are ceremonies and types, and there is a spirituality based upon the types. The new is dark-

ness without its old counterpart, the old is deeper darkness without its new duplicate. If total depravity is declared in the days of Noah, it is reiterated in the days of Peter; if salvation by faith is prefigured in the sacrifice of Abel, it is essentially corroborated by Paul; if immortality is certain to Job, amid his dust and ashes, it has its verification among the visions of John on Patmos; if Abraham made sacrifice in righteousness of faith on Moriah, the world of believers have their Victim on the hill of Calvary; if a GOD in his infinite benevolence saved righteous Lot from a burning Sodom, so the same Being with the same disposition to man saved the Christians who flew to the mountains in the destruction of Jerusalem. The same doctrine of rewards and punishments opens Genesis and closes Revelation. There is no new departure, no inconsistent insertion, no destructive repeal, no amendment, veto nor suppression. This oneness astonishes and proclaims a GOD. Each earlier book supposes an addition ; the parts are unfinished; there is historical harmony; there is prophetical necessity for fuller revelation. Israel's history in Egypt has its sequel in Canaan; the Israel of Canaan is the Captive of Babylon; the same is dispersed over earth from the final destruction of his capital. This new history begins with the purpose of moving to completion a vast system, harmonious, yet simple in its plan and complex in its parts. This unity of facts gives credibility and omnipotence to the impression of a one DEITY who revealed the entire book to "Holy men who spake as they were moved by the HOLY GHOST."

3. *The richness of the Bible message is divine.* Men impress their books with their natures and their thoughts, so that to a familiar reader, the words and sayings of an author become sources of recognition. Look at this Bible! Whose style is displayed? Whose nature is portrayed? Not that of any man; it is peculiar, inimitable, it stands alone. Its undercurrent of virtue is superhuman. Human excellence is inculcated; benevolence is enjoined; charity is commanded; self denial is insisted upon; humility is preached; integrity is exhorted; morality is fostered; innocence is urged; forgiveness is commended and disinterested love is made the highest virtue. The pure judgment and enlightened conscience of every mortal, must approve its code as pure, chaste, virtue-inspiring, peace-producing. All books of to-day that

have similar commendations are simply reflections of the Bible. As an original system without a model it stands unrivaled. Other books are tainted with the age, fashions, prejudices, policy, politics, purposes, plans and habits of the author's home, and are consequently imperfect, partial, perishable. But the Bible was the first book strictly original, never growing old nor superseded, but adapted to all time. The style, language and figure of the Bible are pure as its morals. The oriental, bathed in sunny skies and perfumed atmosphere, lives a poetical life. The Bible, taking its origin under those skies and amid that lovely atmosphere, is clothed in metaphor and parable, fresh with illustrations and spiced with the savory diction of that beautiful land. Its truths go home to the soul for they win their way. Does the emotional nature love to be consulted? Then go to the Bible, for it leads into the picturesque of nature, the pathetic of feeling, the sublime of vision, and the rapt melody of song. Now it storms over the heart with terrible strokes of authority, now it undermines by its profound wisdom and skill, now it besieges by the countermarching of its penalties, and now it takes into sweet captivity by the blessed, tender messages of its love. These remarkable parts that overwhelm, are not found sparse, like diamonds, in the Bible, nor occasionally, like the brightest stars, but they absolutely make the entire book, one pure, powerful, divine mover of humanity. The Bible invites men to a probation of faith, which will really make them better, happier and more prosperous. No special reward is given to corruptly purchase; its rewards are every blessing without money and without price. Human motives rise to the surface, and human schemes are based upon motives, but here men are led to prosperity and happiness without pay. Such imparting without receiving would render bankrupt any one but the Possessor of all things. But the Bible is richer in promises than in all else. The thousand million souls of earth, multiplied by the hundreds of generations that have preceded them and the untold generations that will follow, are all filled with promises the most extraordinary, eliciting hopes the most ardent. Either the Bible is a very wicked book and those trusting its promises come to despair, or it is a divine book and its believers rise to higher hope as they recede from earth; but its believers do all enjoy increasing hope in fruition, therefore the Bible is divine. It promises an immortality of joy; it promises a resurrection, a city of mansions, a transportation of the souls and bodies of men to the city of mansions; it promises most beatific prospects and angelic company. The very conception of its promises is superhuman. It is too violent and incredible for an imposter to propose such grand resurrection displays, such earth-escaping, ether-bearing chariots, and such celestial beatitudes as excite the Christian. False creeds like Mohammedanism, would appeal to the carnal, the material, the nearly approachable. Human creeds would exact heavy material tribute from their dupes. But the promises and conceptions of the Bible, rise up as the love of divinity itself to heaven, and spread out over heaven, filling it.

4. *The Bible Miracles are the highest proof of its divine origin.* Webster says "A miracle is a deviation from the known laws of nature." There is a boundary between the natural and the supernatural which debars the passage of man. But if a God, making all things, exists, he may suspend his own laws, or deviate to produce some wise result, especially to convince the faith of man. The com-

motion of miracles stirs the entire atmosphere of the Bible. The flood with its awful lesson was conviction to Noah; Lot believed when the city of his habitation smoked in ruin: a voice from the sky adopted Abraham; Moses was convinced by the unconsumed bush that had in it a burning God; the Hebrews believed at the terrible plagues upon Egypt, the divided sea, the smitten rock, the falling manna, the smoking Sinai, the dividing Jordan, the vanquished Jericho. But time would fail to tell of the fallen host of Sennacherib, the angel armies around the mountains of Dothan, the ascending Elijah, the glory which filled Solomon's temple, the lions about Daniel, the furnace of fire, the star in the east, the dove at the Redeemer's baptism, the wine of Cana, the five loaves and a few little fishes, the risen Lazarus, the walk on the sea of Galilee, the resurrection from the dead, the Pentecost, the midnight song with the bursting prison doors, and hundreds of other miracles which fill the pages with wonder, the heart with faith, and the world with fear. Many of these miracles were before multitudes and they do not attempt to discredit them, but palliate their force by misrepresentations and confront the rising dead with unbelief, as it is this day. Their forcibleness is indubitable from the cloud of witnesses who attended most of them, the almost entire harmony of explanations, the unanimity of the impartial, and the limitation of prejudice to the most wicked and obdurate, full of selfish ends or restrained by official threats. Only the candid and reliable, and these in myriads, testify as one voice, to the chief miracles of the Bible. No possible explanation can be substituted for the power of a God. Infidelity has poured out the wicked devices of all ages, but its torrents have rendered more fruitful of faith, just as falling showers do not wash away the world, but increase its productiveness. The sun, abiding in mid-day, motionless for twenty-four hours, was witnessed by two armies. The rod of Moses over the Red Sea and the dying host were all seen by three million souls, and Miriam's song reveals the conviction of the rescued Israel, no man daring to make denial. The twelve baskets full of fragments from the broken loaves, which would not before fill one basket, were seen by the seven thousand. The risen Jesus was seen of five hundred. Chance and wily deception never move the sun of the heavens, nor weep the seas into a heap, nor multiply loaves, nor awake the dead. The sun is eight hundred thousand miles in diameter, but it was made to stand still.

> " Should God again
> As once on Gibeon, interrupt the race,
> Of the undeviating and punctual sun,
> How would the world admire!"

A daylight funeral is made for the dead Lazarus in Bethany. The incarnate CHRIST comes and weeps and then, commands.

> " Come forth, He cries, thou dead,
> O God what means that strange and sudden sound
> That murmurs from the tomb?
> That ghastly head,
> With funeral fillets bound?
> It is a living form,
> The loved, the lost, the won,
> Won from the grave, corruption, earth and worms;
> And is not this the son of God!
> They whispered while the sisters poured
> Their gratitude in tears, for they had known the Lord."

The miracles were open, before the multitudes; they appealed to the sight, the hearing and the touch of all; full histories of them were made immediately, by friends and enemies, and continue until this day. Were a miracle to produce a conviction of its probability, the result would be valuable, but were it to overwhelm and bury every doubt in an ocean of certainty, then were undeviating faith the only alternative. Such is the surplus power of the Bible miracles, which, like the top of every living tree of the forest, point up to GOD. Natural laws must yield to the higher and firmer laws of a power above nature. The earthquake is momentous and sudden, the lightning flash startles into awe, but in miracles, without precedent, to flash forcibly convictions of *One God* the sun stands, fire is harmless, water rolls back as a cloud, death yields to life, storms sink into peace on Galilee, armies melt like snow and men ride to glory in chariots of fire. Who is able for these things? It must be a GOD. If this be not GOD, then the laws of sense, of judgment, of faith have been wildly tossed and man has been a raving lunatic, reason has reeled into insanity, the eye is a cheat, the ear a monster of falsehood, and some greater miracle has deceived the whole race of men, in pitiable mockery, to believe, in their insanity, that they were sane, when they were really crazy brutes. If there be no GOD and no miracle, then the cattle of the hills and beasts of the forest that also behold these prodigies of wonder, but without agitation, are sane and rational, while man who beholds and is moved in astonishment and driven to new action—man alone is the senseless, demented, uncaged, wild animal; living and dying in delusive fancy! But no! the faith of man, based on the wonders of the *Elohim* and the *Logos*, greets the Book of books and through it beholds the MIGHTY GOD.

5. *The Bible proves God in the persistence of its believers in all ages.* They died in the faith. Their dying words and hopes are persistent; their testimony is our surety; their physical death is our spiritual life. In belief of the Bible's GOD, they build arks of Gopher wood; they wander in distant lands from the inheritance of fathers; they rally from slavery to freedom over deserts and death; they leave the quiet fisheries of Galilee and go into all the world, telling their faith to every creature, and die violently to seal the sincerity and the candor of their testimony. In this conviction Isaiah was sawn asunder, Jeremiah probably stoned to death, JESUS crucified, and Peter also, with head downward, by preference when feeling his unworthiness, Paul was beheaded, Andrew, tied to a cross with cords, died in protracted tor-

ture, James the Great was beheaded, Philip was hanged to a pillar, Matthew was probably slain with a halbert, St. Thomas was shot through with darts and pierced with a lance, James the Less was thrown from the pinnacle of the temple, then stoned and finally dispatched with a club, Simon probably wandered as an itinerant into Britain and died of crucifixion, Mark suffered Martyrdom, Barnabas and Stephen were stoned to death. But time would fail to speak of Polycarp, Latimer, Ridley, Wickliffe, and the hundred and forty and four thousand who came up through great tribulation. Either the Bible has a GOD, or the Bible-believing, martyred multitude has died in delusion. No explanation is satisfactory of a martyr's conduct, unless some God send this encouragement:— "Be thou faithful unto death and I will give thee a crown of life."

6. *God is made known through the Bible by its enemies.* Profane history, the work of its enemies, is testimony. Cyrus the Persian, who, according to Daniel, captured Babylon, is a well-known monarch of twenty four centuries ago. The Artaxerxes of the Bible is a prominent king of history. Every history of every age, which has come in con-

tact with the Jew, has pictured him as the identical Jew of the Bible, "the Peculiar People," the inheritor of Canaan, the slave in Egypt, the captive of Babylon, lapsing finally into the Pharisee, Sadducee and Essene of later date. Ancient histories are now written from the ancient records and annals of the nations. Monuments and tablets, inscriptions and tombs, relics and ruins conspire with the few written records, and the evidence is deemed complete. The Jew rejects the New Testament and is therefore an enemy. His testimony is valuable as a concession. Josephus, eighteen and a half centuries ago says, "Now there was about this time Jesus, a wise man, if it be lawful to call him a man, for he was a doer of wonderful works, a teacher of such men as receive the truth with pleasure. He drew over to him both many of the Jews and many of the Gentiles, He was Christ. And when Pilate, at the suggestion of the principal men among us, condemned him to the cross, those that loved him at the first did not forsake him, for he appeared to them alive again the third day, as the divine prophets had foretold these and ten thousand other wonderful things concerning him. And the tribe of Christians, so named from him, are not extinct to this day." Such is the corroboration of an enemy eighteen centuries ago. Then came Tacitus, Suetonius, Pliny, Trajan, Martial, Celsus, and other scores who wrote both Latin and Greek, and incidentally disclosed corroborations of enemies to the historical claims and miraculous wonders of the Bible. The best testimony is that forced incidentally from an enemy. Both the Jew and the Christian, scattered as they were when history first pens the events of the world, are found as the Bible indicates, the former involuntarily banished from Jerusalem, the latter voluntarily going from Jerusalem into all the world "to preach the gospel to every creature." Now let us use this testimony. If the Bible be a true book, it is a book whose claims are true; but we have proven that its internal, collateral and profane evidences make it necessarily authentic and true, therefore its claims are true. But it claims to come from God; therefore God exists, the author of the Bible is God, and he lives. The Bible assumes his existence, and really it needs no more proof of its author than do the shrewd dramas of Shakspeare require a series of proofs of the existence of Shakspeare.

7. *The foretelling and fulfillment of prophecy proves a God.* Prophecy is the predicting or foretelling of events before they transpire. It implies a reserve plan and power, as well as a foreknowledge; plan to embrace the future, power to execute, and foreknowledge to disclose. This ability is not human, for futurity is ever a problem to humanity. The curtain of futurity is never lifted, but like a cloud is ever hung up before us. Mortals must wait for to-morrow. We may conjecture, think, imagine, surmise, suspect, fancy when an event is looming in with its phenomena; but the isolated future, the years and centuries hence, no man can know, no being but a God can thus divine. If events centuries distant are revealed to man, the Revelator is the omniscient, omnipresent, eternal God. The Bible claims this for its author, for it is a book of prophecy. Such streams of light come through time to the prophets that events appear just in transition. Names are usually withheld, and the language is skillfully clothed with metaphor, through which spiritual eyes might peer, but wicked and hostile men could never hinder when thus partially concealed—a pillar of a cloud to the wicked, but a pillar of fire to the

righteous. We have seen that the age of a book is evident from its style, the land of its author is mapped from its illustration, the original language is known from its peculiar idiom. These facts and tests render almost indubitable the country, time and language of inspired writers. In the Bible is the prophecy of destruction to cities and kingdoms. Petra in ruins, the capital of ancient Edom, may from its fallen grandeur, point to a GOD who centuries before its fall, proclaimed, "O thou that dwellest in the clefts of the rocks * * I will bring thee down from thence." The pilgrim among the ruins to day may see

"Pillar and arch, defying times' rude shock,
Gleam on each side, upstarting from the rock."

Jerusalem, amid the cold oblivion of its tombs and rocky deeps, was warned of her coming destiny. Tyre, older than Solomon's temple by centuries, the glory of the seas, was wept over by the prophets in her prosperity, and ages afterward destruction felled her in one sweeping blast. The beautiful Palmyra, proud and selfish, had offended DEITY, the prophets warned, time rolled on, and soon it was all faded; it was still strange and grand in its death. Babylon, defiant and impregnable in its massive walls, proud of the captivities it had dictated, was defiant. But behold! solemn predictions discovered its howling ruins. Years fell to decay; but in the full time, undying DEITY rolled Babylon into wild chaos. The ancient Nineveh repented at Jonah's words, but later she sinned; and Nahum and Ezekiel told her destiny, and lo! she too went into the common desolation, But time would fail to tell of the departed glory of Egypt, Persia, Græcia, Assyria, Judæ and the House of Israel.

What voice broke the silence to Abraham? "Thy seed shall be as the stars, and in it shall all the nations of the earth be blessed." Solemn, sublime prophecy! Four hundred and fifty years later, Abraham's seed numbered a million souls, and later still, six or seven millions. Canaan was to be their possession; and on the strength of that prophecy the patriarch made there a family burying ground, four centuries before the host marched over Jordan to the possession. But some voice of God from the sky kept pouring in prophetical words of that "seed of Abraham," Jacob and David; down the ages comes the voice; seven centuries in advance, Isaiah describes the "seed of the Covenant," the Son of God, the "Wonderful, Counsellor, Prince of Peace;" now Daniel, by the streams of captivity, saw the "Messiah" of seventy weeks" hence; and now Malachi beholds the Messenger of John, and the "Sun of righteousness." Every prophet was instructed by a GOD in some circumstance of the coming CHRIST, until the time was apparent; his place of birth, Bethlehem, was known to the prophet, and his nature, mission, kingdom and sacrifice were all pre-figured in a flood of prophetical light; expectation was ablaze, and Jewry groaned for the Deliverer. When lo! "The voice of one crying in the wilderness," the man of "Locusts and wild honey," prepared, as a morning star ushers day, for the splendid fulfillment of prophecy. Then in the lustre of moral day the Redeemer stands before the world. He was called "JESUS" for the prophecy had named him seven hundred years before; he was boundless in charity, for so it was foretold; he was the type of meekness, for so it was predicted; he was a king in righteousness, for to David it was foretold; he blessed the world in his death and his helping grace, for so it was foretold to Abraham two thousand years before. This is the pivot of prophecy:

"O who shall paint Him? Let the sweetest tone
That ever trembled on the harps of heaven
Be discord! let the chanting Seraphim,
Whose anthem is eternity, be dumb,
For praise and wonder, adoration, all
Melt into muteness, ere they soar to Thee,
Thou sole perfection! Theme of countless worlds."

The prophecy which, above all others, glows in power and glory, is the spread of the Church over the earth. This is the day of the Gentiles; Daniel saw it as "The stone cut out of the mountains without hands" filling the whole earth. Isaiah is refulgent in almost every chapter with clear prophecy of Zion's enlargement; the "desert shall rejoice and blossom as the rose." All prophecy culminates in predictions of the spread of Christianity, assuring us of its trials and triumphs peacefully won in GOD'S name. Mark the fulfillment. At the crucifixion all had fled; a little later the eleven saw the risen JESUS, and he established the Church; later one hundred and twenty souls rejoiced in salvation; then came the first public preaching; the first day's work was three thousand souls; then over the seas, and up the mountains, and across the deserts the power of faith arose and the power of a GOD came down; the thousands grew into millions, and the millions are to day the unfolding Church of GOD; a unit of power and influence. Four hundred millions of earth are now controlled by the influence of the Bible. Those millions have a voice of authority which is reaching the remaining millions. Their influence is felt in legislation, on the throne, in the commerce of the seas, in the law-abiding prosperity and industry of the land, in the massive educational movements of nearly all lands, in the restraints of passion and the prevalence of peace among the nations, in the dispersion of darkness and despotism. How signal the progress! on it is going! up it is rising! boundlessly it is prevailing! triumphantly, like the eternal hills, it is culminating! built upon a Rock, thousands of years, it has been spreading, conquering, exulting, advancing, shining, loving, saving! We know not what prophecy is yet to open in the culminating moral day of the Church; but even now prophetical truth abolishes infidelity from truthful inquirers and fills with the faith that climbs to DEITY. The Church is not human; it condemns the human, and has waged long, ceaseless war with the human. Thus has all Bible prophecy become, as reality, an exponent of GOD.

Is there a GOD in the Bible? Yes; the Bible is created by the movings of the HOLY GHOST; the Pentateuch teems with incontrovertible testimony; the Prophets glitter with internal and external evidences; the Gospels cannot but be divine; and Revelation closes the wondrous certainty. The long ages of its messages, the pure, imperishable unity of its life, the harmony of its doctrines, the vast wisdom of its schemes, the wonderful of its promises, the amazingly inexplicable of its miracles, the deathless persistence and faith of its believers, the evident corroboration of its historical supports, and the faithful fulfillment of its prophecies all point up with certainty to a Sovereign Author, GOD.

CHAPTER V.

THE GOD OF THE SPIRIT'S WITNESS, OR THE HOLY SPIRIT EVIDENCES.

COMING from without the spiritual temple, let us kneel before the Shekinah within. We reach from the external to the experimental and the internal, from faith to knowledge. We have appealed to the eye, GOD seen in His works, to the ear, GOD heard in his words, we now appeal to the understanding and the heart, GOD felt in the affections and known in the adoption. Heretofore we reasoned upon the circumstantial, making high probabilities, now we reason upon certainties. This evidence of a GOD is not to the unconverted, apostate, or infidel, but to those in the adoption. In the candor, honesty and integrity of the faithful, the faithless may rest testimony.

Is there then a God who can bear witness with His Spirit?

Observe the world's condition. It lies struggling, groaning, perishing, fearing, hating, dying. The heart has evil thoughts, deceitfulness, every possible wrong of conception, falsity of doctrine, monstrosity of action. Yet with all these, the man lives; he stalks out a probation; he gropes onward to some final destiny; he longs for some Great Physician; he pants for deliverance; he cries in guiltiness.

He has conscience. It will not fully be content with the general stupor. It appeals, threatens with death, warns to amendment, cries aloud for reform, pleads and moves. The whole energy is evil, but so much the more conscience lifts its voice.

The man in desperation appeals to law, and the response is death; the law lifts a burning, blasting voice, it is the decalogue. What bitter consolation is the law! Its spirit, at least, is broken daily. What a wretched hope for the moralist! What a comfortless system for the infidel! If even the Mosaic law be escaped, then a similar law is in our members, full of penalty and condemnation. The law is incompetent in the death dealing disease of sin. From it turn, retreating, routed, flying, both head and heart. God is entreated to avert the horror of Sinai. Its hope is a moral *reductio ad absurdum.*

The soul wanders, weeps and cries, "Who shall deliver us?" Shall atheism? No, that is intolerable soul suicide. Shall infidelity? No, that is the eternal war of the desperate against the omnipotent. Shall formality? No, that is heartless in this fatal fall. Shall indifference and inaction? No, that is inevitable death. "Who then shall deliver?" Some monster absorbs and feasts on the dying soul, and gluts, gnaws and thrives upon the carcass of spirit.

Is there no God to help? Behold a shower like manna falling in the night from heaven!—New-Testament hopes, evangelical instructions, divine invitations, Holy Ghost promises, Christ-inspiring impulsions, attractions, resolutions, gospel-stirring actions, heaven-lifting exaltations. What means this? There must be a God; he comes; and this is his grace and its concomitants.

Now the heart prays, hopes, repents, lingers among the promises, receives the grace, opens the avenues, casts out the unbelief, accepts the plan, believes, lives. Now it rejoices, freely shouts, is full of hope, has immortality, knows, is *justified.*

Where now is the law? dead. Where is condemnation? dissipated. Where is despair? buried in the new tomb of Joseph of Arimathea. Where is sin? canceled by the victim of Gethsemane. Where is death? conquered by the Lion of the tribe of Judah.

Such evidence of a GOD, is like rain in the desert, like bread in the death famine, like sudden summer in winter, like blessed home to the lost, like blooming day in polar night, like the poor orphan dying among strangers, suddenly restored to brother, sister, father, mother.

Others may be persuaded there is a GOD of works and wonders; others may accept external and surface evidence; but this adopted son or daughter has the final and fullest certainty. He knows; it is the *Witness of the Spirit.*

Away with the cold testimony of the stars of heaven and the rocks of earth. They have, it is true, an indubitable inference of a power-GOD; but here at the cross and the mercy seat is the knee of GOD, a talk, a communion, a loving reconciliation, a glorious spiritual day of abiding noon. The soul has found its Father; the flesh has found its Brother; the Spirit of man witnesses with the Spirit of God. It no longer depends upon judicial induction, moral assumption, probable conjecture or hypothetical problems; it rests on experimental certainty, demonstrated reality, absolute knowledge, categorical necessity.

Other evidence aroused faith which brought us from the mountain of legal death to the mercy seat of spiritual life: and God's existence was no longer faith, but knowledge. Faith still has a work, but God now being known, faith is transferred to other duties.

The Spirit being Witness and Companion, all providences, however mysterious or painful, are reckoned blessings in disguise. To the beloved in adoption, sickness and health, prosperity and adversity, life and death, tribulation and anguish, all work together for good. As all the mechanical powers may be combined into one force, as downward, horizontal and angular forces may be concentrated over a pulley which moves all in one combined force upward, so adversities and hindrances fasten upon the believer's golden chain which is flung over the pulleys in yonder sky, and while all these powers of darkness pull downward, the other side of the chain rises, and on it the adopted children climb to heaven.

As the chemist may combine noxious and poisonous gasses and solids into a compound, harmless, sweet and salutary, so now some divine Chemist combines affliction, tribulation and anguish with the experience of the saints, and the result is blessed spiritual expansion and happy communion.

To the original stock of faith and grace is an increase so bountiful and overwhelming that the Christian becomes the richest man in the world. Such an income no Spanish goldhunter, nor merchant on sea or land, nor speculator in ships or railroads could ever reach. It is the imperishable riches, the interest on heavenly capital, the fruit of the Spirit.

Is there no GOD to pour these riches down? No GOD to bring them bubbling up from the fountains of new hearts? Is it simply a good freak of human nature, weaving the beautiful cocoon of morality, and expecting to come out the chrysalis of an angel? There are positives in the evidences of a GOD, love, joy, peace, long-suffering, gentleness, goodness, faith, meekness, temperance, celestial fruits on earthly ground, heavenly seed in hearts made suitable by GOD's grace. What wonderful changes! what miracles of power and goodness! To take a sinner from the arms of the devil and make him sit teachable at the feet of a Risen Jesus, is a miracle more God-like than making or destroying a world. This is the uniform effect of some divine afflatus upon believers.

The divine proofs, presence and interposition are no less potent and convincing when we examine the successive states of exaltation to which the Christian is raised. The Spirit's witness begins at *Conversion.* That there is a speaking-GOD then, is the solemn, certain, miraculous, heart-reaching, joy-producing, soul-satisfying knowledge of every convert. When a voice says "Thy sins are forgiven thee," the sound does not come by the tympanum of the ear, the lips of DEITY are not seen to move by the eye, the knees of the FATHER-GOD are not to be literally embraced by the arms; but, being a heart change the information is communicated directly to the heart with holy assurance. It is like the kiss of a mother, the embrace of affection, the smile of reconciliation, the silent reception of inexhaustible riches with indisputable deeds and titles never to expire nor be lost by contingency. To bring proof to such an one of a GOD would be like proving to him that he has a mother who is then loving him, or a father who is then feeding him.

This is a new relation of man, a new creature. It is an initiation into a new life. The broken and scattered rays are now traced to their origin, the obstructions are removed, and man finds a GOD. This is termed PARDON, JUSTIFICATION. GOD was offended; CHRIST died in righteous satisfaction and pleads his own death merit; man repents and accepts CHRIST'S death and intercession by faith, and now, GOD, moved by mercy to man, intercessory pleadings of CHRIST, and satisfaction in the atonement, writes pardon on the heart. Then the saved sinner knows there is a GOD, for his heart touches the divine heart. The man stands as did Abraham in righteousness by the imputation of faith.

The witness speaks again: it is a cotemporaneous and co-ordinate work with the former and is called REGENERATION. It is the peculiar work of a GOD; it is evidence of him. It is a disposition wrought within by some power, evidently the same that brought the former gift. It delivers from sin's dominion, prompts to new action by the full freedom of the will and inclines to happy and constant service to GOD. Watson says, "Justification is a change of position, but regeneration is a change of disposition." Sin is abolished and power is infused to think, feel and do, inwardly and outwardly the pleasure of a GOD. This is not the work of man or devil, nor can it be a delusion of its possessor; but it is a powerful, holy, divine work. The bad, once loved, is now hated; the good, once hated, is now loved. There is exaltation in practice and impulsions. Such a man loves GOD because he loves to love him and hates sin because he loves to hate it. This work is a wonderful evidence of DEITY'S existence.

A third time the witnessing voice speaks and the magic result is ADOPTION. Man had been an alien and enemy, his heirship was forfeited and his sonship lost. And yet the wandering prodigal was restored by re-instatement. It could not be the result of our rights, works or merits, but the result of a joint heirship with CHRIST, the true heir. The channel of our movement was not direct, but we became sons of GOD because CHRIST is, and he insists upon mercy like an elder brother. Servitude and fear go, and freedom and love come. Distrust is abolished, confidence is established. Free, holy communion takes the place of guilty retreats and concealment. Eternal inheritance is certainty and being is pervaded and overwhelmed by a joy which cries "Abba Father." It is a new revelation of the Holy Ghost, comforting, clear, certain. It is a miraculous energy condescending in acknowledgement to tell us plainly that we are of the family circle of GOD. When GOD speaks it is direct and positive, though within. To the direct is added human testimony; the recipient corroborates. Ask the man who has the Holy Ghost to witness adoption, whether he has a conformable love and harmony in the divine. This is co-ordinate testimony. Consciousness becomes a moral intuition, newly begotten, centering the fact of adoption in the soul. Does the child of GOD doubt his Father's existence? No, GOD lives to pet, love and delight in his children.

A fourth time some holy GOD utters a voice and with it comes the highest blessing earth's wanderer has on earth. It is CHRISTIAN PERFECTION, SANCTIFICATION, or HOLINESS. This voice, though positive, has not been heard by all the Church. In conformity to the Bible invitation, believers may "go on to perfection," "be holy," "be cleansed from all sin." These commands have the same authority as the Bible, and duty is clearly inculcated. Believers may, by prayer, faith and constant growth in grace, approximate indefinitely near this state of perfection, yet the scriptural doctrine designates this as a new and glorious installment, the last and best which the Bible's GOD can speak to man in the flesh. Nor is it a gift of some purgatory after death, or a gift only attainable at and by death, but it is a blessing in waiting for all Christians, young and old. Sanctification presupposes the humble, willing, believing soul, asking to be shut in God from sin or sinful tendency, and to have that positive, immaculate purity of heart, life and love that will make the saint walk with GOD perfectly, free from sin and in holy joy. The legal act is GOD's act. The Holy Ghost accepts this entire heart and sweetly communicates the witness and the word that seals the covenant. "GOD is love," but the fearing, doubting Church is lulled into quietness and its power and influence are fearfully decimated. When we see the sanctified soul however, we must see GOD; two walking so closely together are either both concealed or both revealed. Death is but a translation, to the sanctified.

Thus we see there is a GOD in the life of the Christian from pardon to perfection. Prisons do not hinder the communion; bonds are no barrier; poverty does not exclude the heavenly treasure from the earthen vessel; exile does not separate from GOD; persecutions cannot alienate the two witnesses; devils cannot frighten from GOD; principalities and powers are too feeble to put asunder the adopted son from the Heavenly Father; death itself, the terrible disorganizer of all else, only loosens the soul from its bonds and earth hails it no more when started on the deathless flight to be forever with GOD.

THE GOD OF PRAYER'S ANSWER INVOKED.

CHAPTER VI.

THE GOD OF PRAYER'S ANSWER.

TYNDALL was subtle in his infidel refinements when his mode of testing prayer was propounded. Not whether a GOD will hear prayer made without the conditions of prayer, and simply made in faithless experiment to gratify an infidel, but whether a GOD was ever known to hear prayer in the history of any person, or of the Christian Church, is the true and only logical or theological test question. Was Tyndall more consistent in his recent infidel address in England? The first mode is cunning sophistry, it would be assuming a universal conclusion from particular premises. Its only equal was once heard from the pinnacle, rather than the pulpit of the temple, saying "If thou be the son of GOD cast thyself down from thence." "Thy will" is omitted, and all temporalities are assumed as pertinent tests of certain answer, the divine will being ignored. But the true test is this,

DID A GOD EVER ANSWER A PRAYER?

The man who descended into a deep coal mine was, before starting, instructed, if he desired anything below, when in the basket that was suspended by cords under the windlass, to ring the bell or pull the signal cord. He had the promise of certain aid from the man at the windlass, and would have indubitable proof that the man was there. In this manner, a mortal in distress may make the signal prayer; it is answered; help comes; and it brings assurance that an almighty hand is at the windlass of the universe.

Prayer's answer is a positive proof of a GOD's existence, and far more, it proves His attributes. The blessings of the atonement, and the testimony of internal joy and external favor realized were preceded by prayer. The invitation to pray is made through the Bible to those who have faith. Its condition pre-supposes human want, divine abundance, and the theory that human want is relieved in the divine abundance as indirect answer to prayer. Such is the evangelical dogma. Why it is so, we will not, we cannot explain. It is GOD's plan; this is enough. Nor could it be so, if divine decrees were irrevocable. It can be true only when the divine plan to us-ward is left impressible to human prayer. No other theory is conceivable. As absurd as the above is all possible prayer on the supposition that no GOD exists.

The theory of prayer being agreed upon, we must appeal to the practice for experimental evidence of GOD. Millions have sought blessings in prayer in all ages, and the blessings came. The infidel may assert that general results would come to all alike, with or without prayer, making prayer void. Such assertion supposes what has been, as inevitable and unmodified, and yet prayer may have modified and revolutionized the entire course of events. We answer the objection by this assertion, that without prayer and its answer the world would have been moral chaos, or the race would more likely have been cut off long ago. But our test of a GOD is rather found in those striking and unquestionable answers, and especially in spiritual things. "Behold he prayeth" is the first gleam of hope to the fallen. The converted man found his blessing by prayer; the progressive Christian started and moved upward by the power of prayer; marked afflictions, if triumphantly endured, were conquered in a victory of prayer; and whoever has risen through great tribulation, or gone to reward through martyrdom has procured triumph in prayer.

The humble sinner sent a prayer upward; it did not fall back upon him, but instead a voice came saying: "Son, daughter, thy sins are forgiven thee;" then another voice said, "Ask largely that your joy may be full." The soul obeys; and the voice again says, "Thy prayers are answered; thou art precious." Now what voice is this? Is it the floating wind, playing upon the ear? No, it plays upon the heart. Is it some loose, free angel or departed spirit flying through the air, arresting the words of the praying one and whispering answers in idle pranks of deception? No, it is inconceivable that a good angel or saint would deceive, and for a bad angel, it is too powerful, holy, and abiding. It must be the soul's Father; it must be the Bible's God; for every answer comes in compliance with the Bible plan, every experience confirms the Bible theory, every enjoyment is a revelation of Bible promises, and every answer to prayer is a satisfactory test of the Bible's GOD.

The daily answer to the daily prayer of one Christian is proof of a GOD; add to the one, the answers to the millions in all the earth, which float down like a sea of glory to overwhelm, and bathe, and bless, and you prove an omnipresent GOD; add the prayers of all ages, full of peaceful answers to the living and the dying, and you have an eternal GOD; add the mighty answers that have brought miracles and wonders, parching drouths and rushing storms, that have brought fire from heaven to lick up water, that have displayed angelic legions and burst prison doors, and you have an omnipotent GOD.

In chemistry one experiment testifies with certainty to an invisible element, and no man denies it, but in our experimental theology of prayer, the infinite number of tests that fill the ages with momently multiplied accumulations, do prove a DEITY on his throne of mercy in all time, full of all perfection of attributes and crowned with beauty, truth, and grace.

Is prayer answered in heaven? The Bible is full of recorded testimony of availing prayer. Ask

Jonah, as by prayer he escapes from the fish; ask Solomon whose temple in dedication was filled with glory; ask Daniel whose prayer still lingering on his lips, had blessed answer through Gabriel; ask Nehemiah, whose way was opened, in reply to prayer, for rebuilding the walls of Jerusalem; ask the devout Cornelius who saw free grace offered to the Gentiles; ask Peter as he walks alive and free in company with angels from Herod's prison; ask the incarnate host who got strength at the mercy seat of earth to rise to the mansions of heaven.

> "Once they were mourners here below,
> And poured out cries and tears."

Noted answers to prayer fill the records of the devout. Melancthon was dying and rejoiced in the near deliverance, but Luther regarding that the Church could not possibly spare him prayed earnestly one hour for his life, and they both believed it was continued in answer. When Shleiswick was invested by savage Cossacks, a mother in the suburbs prayed for a wall of defence. Dreary snow was falling, winds howled, darkness fell, the hideous foe came but did not enter the house of prayer. It was inexplicable until morning, when the snow-wall high up around the dwelling, by angel hand, in answer to a mother's prayer, determined the problem.

Prayer is answered; by whom? By the Christian's God. It is holy proof of "Our Father in heaven." At the consecrated mercy seat down comes the tender, hope-lifting, blessing-bearing voice of a God reconciled to the praying heart. It comes in the closet, in the family circle, in the public congregation. The answer comes in battle-field, and the peace and protection of God make the soldier proof against bayonet or bullet, when the fervent prayer of loving wife or aged mother has moved God. Each Christian reader has had the prayer proof of God's existence. In danger, doubt or discouragement you receded from the world, you fell down in prayer; that moment, you struck a vein of the reserve forces of the universe; they were yours; all things were then yours; "Whatsoever" became the broad word of reply; faith arose; blessings fell; you rejoiced, worshiped, praised, was full, had communion with a God, as had the primeval man in the first days of Eden. The highest objective proof of God becomes this subjective reality. "The eyes of the Lord are over the righteous and his ears are open unto their prayers."

> "O the precious privilege to the pious given—
> Sending by the dove of prayer holy words to heaven!
> Arrows from the burning sun cleave the quivering air;
> Swifter, softlier, surer, on speeds the dove of prayer,
> Bearing from the parted lips words of holy love,
> Warm as from the heart they gushed to the throne above."

From effect to cause we have risen in these pages. In *Nature* but one cause was possible, and that Cause was God. In *History* the same God was the only conceivable Cause. In *Moral Government* the Same *Cause* was identified again. In the Bible we recognize the same Divine Author. In the *Spirit's Witness* the same God becomes the soul's Father reconciled. And finally in the *Answer to Prayer*, "God is, and is a Rewarder to them that diligently seek Him." This is the sum of our scheme. If its array does not force conviction to the infidel, it still adds to the proof that "Men love darkness rather than light because their deeds are evil." But the man of faith will be assisted to find his God and to worship at his feet.

PART II.

THE FATHER-GOD'S FAMILY.

"Τοῦ γὰρ καὶ γένος ἐσμέν."

"For we are also his offspring."

CHAPTER I.

Composition, Character and Work of God's Family.

THE Family Circle is the hallowed center of earth's best felicity. Silvery are its smiles of encouragement, golden its tenderness in affliction, diamond its treasured forgiveness to the prodigal and the fallen, God-like its abiding love in weal or woe.

To this mystic circle hastens the business man in despair when the fire-fiend sweeps his wealth to ashes, here come the abandoned daughter and the prodigal son, he or she is a weeping child once more where home-love hears all, forgives all, and the fallen is born again into child-like tenderness and love.

The Family Circle begins with the holy joys of the wedding day. Its attractions are enhanced by each young pair of playful hands and pattering feet, each new born tongue to prattle and heart to confide. Babe is the holiest jewel and parent the richest adventurer in the wide world. With parent and children the circle is complete.

"HOME IS THE FAMILY RETREAT."

Home is the family retreat. Father is prophet, priest and king; mother is tender and loving as a spirit which sanctifies; brother and sister are its angels of light; and child is its singing cherub. Its hearthstone is a Holy of holies, where the Angel of the Covenant comes in the hour of prayer; and in the family Bible, pressed lovingly between the old and new Covenants, is the only spot sacred enough for a genealogy of the group. And yet, only a leaf intervenes, and the angel of death has a reserve page, white, blank and cold, waiting the dark record of mourning.

Now this family circle, so like to heaven, is the unfallen symbol of the

FAMILY OF GOD

in this wide universe. All are one SPIRITUAL FAMILY, from the homestead, the "house not made with hands," to the outer fields where the angels reap the harvest; all are members, from the Father of all things on heaven's throne, to the child-man, staying in this world's playhouse until the signal of Gabriel come to gather the family home into eternal joy.

GOD'S family is every creature that has a heart

of charity. Whether it pulsate in the fatherhood of GOD, or throb in the apostleship of angels; whether it beat harmony in the glorified body of saints or vibrate love in the flesh of probative man, it blends creature and Creator into a family.

The aliens of the family are all who hate. Whether the hatred rankle in the breast of hopeless devil or helpless man, still the heart that hates is an alien.

Every inhabitant of earth has a religion. Atheism is found only in Christian lands, and is falsely so called. It is only a retreat of doctrine for convicted sinners, who in advance call for rocks and mountains to fall upon them. The world is divided religiously, by every Geographer and Historian, into Mohammedan, Pagan, Jew and Christian. The nations that are nominally Christianized contain four hundred and fifteen millions of souls or one third of the world. Here is an immense family, whose pilgrimage is from pole to pole and from east to west.

The Historian, and not GOD, further subdivides Christians into

ROMAN, GREEK, AND PROTESTANT.

Let each mouth proclaim to infidelity with GOD'S thunder, that these four hundred and fifteen millions, in three great branches, have one LORD, one faith, one baptism. They all believe man a sinner, GOD in CHRIST a SAVIOUR, faith in CHRIST a redemption, and heaven the eternal home of all believers. Minor differences may divide in part, bodily color may prejudice, national traits, temperaments, education and a thousand minute varieties of the individual may tend to sever, but the great sympathy and doctrines hold all Christendom in a family. Of these three divisions we consider

I. THE ROMAN.

Romanism flourishes in Italy, Spain, Portugal, Austria, and largely in South America, Mexico, Belgium and Ireland. It is intensely missionary. It numbers one hundred and fifteen millions of subjects. It arose at Rome. Heathen Rome, at its foundation, sought, as a national policy, to retain its people at home and to provide a religious theory that would fill the empty, longing heart of Rome with a DEITY. Human inventions and additions were incorporated from time to time with the first rude religion which sprang from policy. After crucifying the Son of GOD and thousands of his immediate followers; after martyring Peter and Paul, in the lapse of a few centuries, the empire gradually passed to Christian Rome. They assumed CHRIST as the head of the Church, Peter whom they had martyred as the first Pope, and the cross as the emblem of their conquering power. Constantine saw in the halo above him a cross, and the words which accompanied proclaimed, "By this conquer." This pretended vision made Rome ever after zealous to enforce the religion of the cross by the might of the sword. Thus the Romish Church, arising as a governmental necessity, reached only the head. The heart unchanged, gushed forth a fountain of corruption, and it was all assimilated with the creeds of the sword. Hence relics, images and saints were worshiped, the Virgin Mary was invoked, purgatory was pacified with Peter's pence, sins were committed with impunity by indulgences or works of supererogation, popes that were earthly, sensual, devilish were regarded infallible. Kings kissed popish toes and fell prostrate to have their necks trod upon and their crowns kicked off by infallible feet. The pope was the only historical vice-gerent of CHRIST for a thousand years. It was a millenium of night. But because GOD in his own time does eliminate every error, and signalize and honor with power and prevalence every truth, the Roman of the dark ages is not the Roman of to-day. Not by any innate truth, power, light or progress, but by the restraining, moving power of GOD and true religion, the Romanist of to-day is forced into a better form of policy and religion. The terror of the mother Church to the martyr has been transformed into stratagem with the intellect. Her authoritative excommunications and bulls are modified into artful diplomacy. Her ecumenical councils do not now meet to burn an incorrigible heretic or other outer foe, but to eliminate her inner corruptions and absurdities and adopt better formulas for the demands of the age. Now political empire must be abandoned; now infallibility, voted by a bare majoity, is a rock of division; now education is urged by the pope and the priest upon every member; now their claim to exclusiveness only elicits the world's sarcastic smile. All this modification is not internal reformation, but external compulsion. Tetzel sells indulgences no more, no idiot will buy. Leo crowns and uncrowns kings no more, no prince consults him; pious monks martyr Christians no more, for the common law would hang such monks as murderers. Bound thus in chains, popery is as mild as a theory of the stars.

By his toleration of Romanism as an organization, thus far, GOD has indicated his permissive providence. It may be better for the civil restraints and the final reformation of the Roman Church, that her organization remain in force as at present, rather than that, to rid the world of her errors, her organization perish, and her people, unrestrained, undirected, despairingly plunge into total chaos. Formal Romanism restrained by Christianity, is far better than heathenism unrestrained. Whether, hereafter, DEITY will annihilate the Roman Church, or sift and reform it, no man can tell. Meantime it is our duty to pray and disseminate the peace of GOD's Son, even among the Romanists. Momentous revolutions are now rapidly solving this problem of the reformation of Romanism. The pope sits powerless and on a chair of vacancy, as unenviable as an old steed turned out to die. The Romanists of Austria have rebelled against infallibility; and the old Mother Church, now sinking into the infirmities of second childhood, is learning wisdom of her children and the Grand-Parent of us all. Father Hyacinth dissents from the pope and fraternizes with Christendom. We may hope that the Roman branch, stripped of error by the power of GOD, will hereafter wheel into the purified ranks of the Church militant, a power for righteousness. GOD can do it, and to this end let us ever in charity pray.

II.

We allude next to the second historical branch of the Christian Church,

THE GREEK.

Pagan Rome persecuted Christianity until the year A. D. 312, when Constantine proclaimed his vision of the Cross, burnished in the sky above him, and the attendant words—"By this Conquer." By this event the Roman empire was converted in a day, but only in policy. The empire was now so weak and yet so wide, that like an ellipse, it had two foci, Rome and Constantinople. The latter was superior, and to it, as the chief center, Constantine was attracted. Thus the birth of Christianity in the Roman Empire was a twin birth, the Romish church with its head at Rome, and the Greek church with its head at Constantinople. Of these, the Greek Sister was the purer minded. It may be because of proximity to Jerusalem where Christ formed the true Church and apostolic teachings more abounded. It may be in part because of removal from the warring, stirring Italy. Though unlike, these Roman and Greek ecclesiastical sisters must needs, in their infancy, be nourished by the same political matrix and the same theological paps. After ninety years, (396 A. D.) the Eastern and Western Empires were severed under Theodosius, *and that moment the Greek Church had its independent life.*

Though alienated and divorced thus from Rome through sectional jealousy and political rivalry, though born as the bastard of the sword and the sceptre, though bred as a thankless, inferior, undesired child of dishonor, yet when the Greek Church separated from the Roman, she had a purer mind, a holier faith, a more evangelical doctrine.

The theological separation from Rome, though begun in 396, was not formally completed until 1054 A. D. The Greek Church disown infallibility and the pope ; they do not grant indulgences; they deny purgatory; they reject auricular confession ; they administer the sacrament to all ;

they exclude confirmation, extreme unction and matrimony out of the sacraments; and they discard the worship of the Virgin Mary. But they do pray for the dead; they do invoke saints, not as gods, but as intercessors; they do accept predestination; their priests do marry before orders; they do accept consubstantiation, or the presence of Christ's body with the bread in the Sacrament.

It will be evident that the Greek church is a religious body decidedly in advance of the Roman. Herein we may know that the revolutions of man become the evolutions of GOD, either directing, controling or restraining human actions, and finally harnessing all force to the mighty train that bears His Church heavenward.

The Greek Church has lost its political cast. The Saracen has possessed Constantinople for ages, but this body of Christians lives on. Millions are its votaries. It conquers and warms the heart of the Russian, who, in his snow-bound empire and arctic fastnesses, is invincible to the world. It smiles on the balmy peninsula of Homer. It pours perennial life in Syria, where GOD'S SON lived and walked and died and ascended. It blesses in Egypt, where Pharaoh perished and Moses triumphed. It shines in Asia Minor where the Seven Candlesticks of the Seven Churches were lighted eighteen centuries ago by Apostolic fire. It saves in Armenia where Adam was lost, and Noah found help until the storm was overpast. It culminates up the mountain sides of Persia, and through its Magi, daily carries new gifts, guided by the Bethlehem star, to worship the ever adorable GOD-MAN of the incarnation. The Nestorian branch in Central Asia, one hundred thousand strong, is keeping the faith, and longs to unite with the missionaries that come in from the south and the east, from India and China, and make a common family circle ot Christian faith all over these ancient homesteads of the race. All this Greek church numbering at least one hundred millions of souls, is a part of the grand and glorious host on earth, GOD'S family.

Tell it again to the sneering infidel of every creed in Christendom; proclaim it aloud to the martial Mohammedan, the sensual Pagan, and the inflexible Jew, that the family of the Crucified JESUS, with a common faith, embraces the Roman host and the Greek host, in all two hundred and fifteen millions. Our GOD'S family, even on earth, is a great multitude, that no man can number.

III.

We consider thirdly the

PROTESTANT

branch of GOD's family. Its origin marks the power of GOD and the almost miraculous invincibility of a man at work under GOD's protection. Michael Angelo, the Painter and Architect, was building the magnificent and costly St. Peter's church at Rome for Pope Leo X. It cost fabulous sums, but the work must go on, and means must be invented to amass money for that object. Popery was capable of inventing the plan. It was the year 1529. Leo was Pope. Charles V. was Emperor of Western Europe. Martin Luther was Professor of Divinity at Wittenberg University, and GOD was on the throne of the Universe.

The Roman Church then believed that pious persons might be so active and so abound in good works, that they would accomplish more than was required, or works of supererogation; and, that these works, together with the infinite merits of JESUS CHRIST, were put into an inexhaustible treasury, and, that the key to this treasury, originally given to St. Peter, had been transferred to each successive pope who could thereby open the treasury and buy a soul from purgatory, or grant another permission to sin all his life. These permissions to sin were called *indulgences*; and the cunning pope, unlike CHRIST, would not grant these indulgences without money and without price, but sold them for an extravagant sum. Here is a copy of the pope's indulgence:

"May our LORD JESUS CHRIST have mercy upon thee, and absolve thee by the merits of His most holy passion. And I, by His authority, that of His blessed apostles, Peter and Paul and of the most holy pope, granted and committed to me in these parts, do absolve thee, first, from all ecclesiastical censures, in whatever manner they may have been incurred; then from all thy sins, transgressions, and excesses, how enormous soever they may be; even from such as are reserved for the cognizance of the holy see, and as far as the keys of the holy Church extend. I remit to you all punishment which you deserve in purgatory on their account; and I restore you to the holy sacraments of the Church, to the unity of the faithful, and to the innocence and purity which you possessed at baptism; so that, when you die, the gates of punishment shall be shut, and the gates of the paradise of delight shall be opened; and if you shall not die at present, this grace shall remain in full force when you are at the point of death. In the name of the FATHER, SON, and the HOLY GHOST."

Here are some of the prices for indulgences in particular sins:—"For Simony, 10s. 6d.; for sacrilege, 10s. 6d.; for taking a false oath, 9s.; for robbing, 12s.; for burning a neighbor's house, 12s.; for defiling a virgin, 9s.; for murdering a layman, 7s. 6d.; for keeping a concubine, 10s. 6d.; for laying violent hands on a clergyman, 10s. 6d."

By these monies St. Peter's Church was to be built. Pope Leo sold to the highest bidder the privilege of selling indulgences, as we sell the right to a territory on a patent. Tetzel acquired the territory of Saxony, and opened the auction for the sale of his indulgences. *At this point the Reformation began.* So absurd and ungodly was the entire scheme, that the aforesaid Luther, monk as he was, exposed the cheat, and aroused all Saxony.—Then, in anathemas and revenge, Rome was aroused, and at last Charles V. and the whole empire as friend or foe. Human elements stormed. GOD was looking down from his throne upon the storm, in due time ready to say "Peace, be still." Luther, like the Lion for terror, the champion for God, was standing firm as adamant. He withstood anathemas and bulls, and made them into bonfires. Perdition rallied its imps, numerous as the very tiles upon the houses. Councils assembled with arms as well as arguments, ready to clash. Meantime the Bible first came to the multitudes and fed them, like the loaves and fishes of a Jesus. Truth flew on wings, and sounded like the voice of God in the tops of the Mulberry trees. Multitudes believed and flew to its standard. Romanism trembled as if a moral earthquake had shattered its spired steeples and its rich Cathedrals to the ground. The final appeal was made by popery to Charles V. A decree was proclaimed which was intended to overwhelm Luther and the reformation. That decree struck them as a gentle zephyr would strike the Rocky Mountains, for God was with them. *Then and there the Protestant division of the Christian family was born.*

Luther and several Princes of Germany *protested* against the decree—hence

PROTESTANTISM.

Luther, Melancthon and others, were the champions of righteousness in Germany, Calvin in

France, Zuinglius in Switzerland, Knox in Scotland. These and thousands became independent witnesses and interpreters of the truth and the Bible. Hence they grouped into sections having a common faith and differing in minor particulars. Hence arose Lutherans, Baptists, Presbyterians, Congregationalists, Methodists and many others. It is not our province, as the manner of some is, to magnify their differences—Satan will do that. The microscope of Charity can see no differences. The harmony and unity of all is the blessed theme of our joy to day.

Individuals may be unfriendly, but these protestant branches are one. Sin which made war and murder and division between the first pair of brothers, would gladly extend the strife to the judgment day. But even the minor differences are dissolving in the heat of charity. In November the Protestants of our broad Union annually hold a common Thanksgiving to Almighty God. In January the Evangelical Alliance of the Protestant world hold a week of prayer in common, to the same Head of the Church, for the same blessings.

The Wesleyan and the Protestant Methodist

branches, and other less numerous Methodist bodies are on the way to unify with the Methodist Episcopal Church. Two Methodist bodies of Ireland are being unified, as well as two of Canada. These are but fore-runners of the entire unification of Methodism; and a few months or years will witness the consummation. The Old and New School Presbyterians, after an alienation of forty years, are again smiling in perfect reconciliation. The Baptist, somewhat persistent in his sacramental exclusiveness, is widening his doors, his arms, his heart. The Episcopalian, so firm in his dogma of apostolical succession, has his Colensos, Dr. Tyngs, Bishop Cheneys and Mc Ilvaines, who are full of charity. This branch has progressed since Henry VIII. and Cardinal Woolsey rebelled against Popes Leo and Adrian. Dogmas and creeds are being rapidly labeled among the fossils of the theological cabinet. The points of agreement are so infinitely greater than the points of difference that they are evidently only varieties of the same family. The Congregationalist, the Baptist, and the Methodist differ less than James, Peter and John, whom our Lord fed at the same table and took to the same heaven.

THE SPIRITUAL FAMILY.

We have thus far considered the nominal or historical family, and have found four hundred and fifteen millions of souls. These are man's figures. God may reckon differently. He counts hearts rather than heads. We have fully confessed the quarrels of the *nominal* family, but the great *spiritual* family, full of regeneration and charity, never quarrels. They are all one in CHRIST JESUS. GOD does not depend upon our History or Geography, nor transfer his account from man's books. Being a nominal Church-member does not initiate into the Spiritual family. "Not every one that saith LORD, LORD, shall enter into the kingdom." Nay, the sanctimonious minister, whose end is to eat loaves and fishes and wear ermine, may be an eternal apostate, while a naked, despised heathen may be fairly upon the poll-list of immortality. The difference between head and heart must be striking, often, to God who can see and compare them.

It is not the province of man to read the heavenly roll of names, nor yet to read the roll of perdition. We may not, by authority, church nor unchurch saint nor sinner. We may not even judge, lest we *be* judged.

But yet Revelation does clearly state the qualities that must be in GOD's children. Whether A B or C have those qualities, the individual and his GOD must determine. We will name some signs of relationship in the spiritual family.

1. *They must be men of faith.*

It is not the faith of formalists nor of devils. It is not an intellectual acceptance of cool dogmas. It is not a frozen feast of mental ice cream.

It is yielding the old heart for the new. It is feeling full of sin and empty of CHRIST until the longing nature is reversed, feeling empty of sin and full of CHRIST. It is losing hold of the straws and shrubs and of self, and taking hold of CHRIST firmly, constantly, believingly. It is a daily feasting upon the promises, when the soul thrives and grows upon its food. It is an hourly spiritual acceptance of CHRIST's righteousness, to the joy and bliss of the nature. It is having CHRIST only, from the new life begun in the soul to the life consummated in the perfections of immortality.

2. *The Spiritual Family have Regeneration.*

That overturns. The old nature moves out, taking all its property, and the new nature moves in with a completely new outfit. This *must* be so.

"Except a man be born again he cannot see the kingdom of GOD." CHRIST proclaims it. There is mystery. But the Spirit does it. Faith and prayer keep that spirit at work. It is looking unto JESUS until the divine image take on the tablet of a believing heart. It is sitting for the picture until these poor negatives may be cast aside and the soul feels it is a new creature. A breeze, soft from the warm south, so gently comes that the flower nodding on the hill is not much stirred by it, but it infuses warmth. "The wind bloweth where it listeth * * So is every one that is born of the Spirit." The solemn work is within. Others may not discover it, as the wind is unseen, but the recipient feels the warmth and knows.

3. *God's family have obedience.*

The Spirit leads them. They are the sons of GOD. Work and suffering mingle our destinies. To *suffer* the Will of God in patience is the heavy task of the afflicted—To *do* GOD's will is the portion of those strong in the regeneration. With powers delegated in man, and duties spread over earth, the human will must be lost, and the will divine must move the worker. The inimitable CHRIST is holding the multitude by His gracious words, when His mother and brethren are announced. Will He pause in His mission to obey the will even of His mother? No. But He interposes this corollary in the sermon; "Whosoever doeth the will of my Father which is in heaven, the same is my brother, and sister and mother." Led by the Spirit was the portion of our LORD to the temptations of the wilderness, and "Led by the Spirit," is the hope of the trusting disciple.

4. *The family of God has Charity.*

This is the highest, holiest, purest symbol of family ties. It is the eloquent peroration of a soul. It is the quintessence of religion, budding, flowering, fruiting in the life. When all conceptions below heaven are compared and weighed, it is greatest. "We know we have passed from death to life, because we love the brethren." "The greatest of these is Charity."

We have mentioned four peculiarities which, if a man have, he is a child of GOD, and of his family. If a man lack these he must be a child of sin. Other traits could be added, but they ever combine with these. Christian graces and traits never live singly, they congregate and populate a heart like a full city.

Men with these traits are known like cities on a

hill, like lights shining. All such are adopted into the family of God. Whether in rags or robes, wealth or want, whether in princes or plebeians, Romanists or protestants, Jews or gentiles, beggars or bankers, they become the pledges and proofs of the spiritual family of God.

When Elijah was discouraged and regarded himself alone as God's servant in all Israel, and actually told God so, God answered, " There are seven thousand of my servants who have not bowed the knee to Baal."

Say *not* that the Spiritual family is less than the Historical family. We are usually not charitable enough. After allowing a liberal discount for apostates, hypocrites, infidels and the finally lost, of Christian lands, we know not but enough will be saved among the heathen and their dying children to fully meet the deficiency.

Tell it once more with the voice of seven thunders, to the skulking, deaf infidel, Jew, Mohammedan, pagan, and every other sinner who chooses the discord of hell before the concord of heaven, that the Christian family that worships Jesus and seeks heaven by faith, is now augmented by the one hundred and fifteen millions of the Roman Church, the one hundred millions of the Greek, and the two hundred millions of the Protestant, a grand army of the living God, four hundred and fifteen million souls. This is the Church Militant; this is the Family of God on earth; this is "Zion the Perfection of Beauty."

They affiliate in *one Father*. They each pray "*Our* Father," not selfishly "*My* Father."

They each sing, "To him that hath washed *us*" —not "*me*". The same Bible is their Lamp. The same nature is their trait of a Peculiar People. The same Pilgrimage is their lot. The same death in Christ is their hope. The same Heaven their Home.

They are intensely missionary. "Go ye into all the world," moves all the moral host, as gravity moves the stars—"Preach the gospel to every creature," flies over the world like flames of light from the sun. "Lo I am with you alway," comes to Romanist, Greek and Protestant, and wraps heaven and power around their naked souls. *Here*, Herbert Spencer, is your co-relation of forces—The conversion of momentum—The Power of God is breathed into a church—That church is soul and body—It has food and raiment, and time, and talent, and Bibles, and the love of souls, and a commission to evangelize the world—and now the "*All Power*" is added—sublime addition of the infinitely great to the infinitely little. This determines the battle; the scale is turned; the everlasting gospel flies; idols break; four millenniums of constant night dawn; grim devils retreat to outer darkness; hell's reserve corner must remain a wilderness depopulated; the Church triumphs; the missionary shouts "Victory! Victory!! Victory!!! The LORD GOD OMNIPOTENT reigneth" And I hear the future voice of the saints and martyrs of all ages, spoken into life, arise from their dusty shrouds, and with glorified bodies catch and carry the sound upward once more, from the missionary echo, "Victory! Victory!! Victory!!! For HE hath redeemed us and made us kings and priests of our GOD forever." And I hear a still higher voice of the angels in the ancient homesteads of heaven catch the shout of the glorified, as it musically rises through the everlasting doors, and all heaven repeats once more, "Victory! Victory!! Victory!!! Glory to the FATHER and to the SON and to the HOLY GHOST, of whom the whole family in heaven and earth are named."

CHAPTER II.

God's Family enter Sleep, or Death.

We have seen, in the last pages, the family of God on earth at work. We have estimated its numbers, its composition, its glory, its achievements, its victory. But the work ends, day fails, shadows lengthen, night comes, darkness gathers. The weary family count the hours, observe the changes, prepare for them and wait the result.

The Spirit Father comes. The angel of death is with him. It is a good but sad angel. Its work makes earth sad and sepulchral, but it also makes heaven near and immortal. This angel is the porter of the gates beyond. God makes the narrow bed, but it was wide enough for Jesus. Father pities the weary, and when He draws the curtains of night and commands stillness there, He wipes away tears and puts His weary children to rest. This is death. As a mother folds the little one in her arms, when it settles in slumber, so the soul's Father encompasses the sleeping dust in the everlasting arms.

Is the man dead now? No, he sleepeth. There is sequence here; there is outgrowth; there is an awakening; there is a future.

The sepulcher is not beautiful, and we may not court a sojourn there. Its object is rest; that attained and the morning light will come. The day is glorious; it is eternal; it is a holiday of gladness in all the family of God. And the same parent that closed the eyes of his children in sleep, now comes again in the morning to awaken them, strip off the cerements, the night dress of mortality and clothe them in the attire of immortality.

This is not all a mystery to natural observation. Vegetables bud and bloom, then the leaf is crimson, and at last, detached from the bough, it bleaches in dust. But the twig germ of to-morrow in the same spot and the shrub of next year proclaim re-animation.

Summer itself is chilled; first yielding to autumnal frost, it is afterwards wholly forgotten in the blasts of winter.

Childhood laughs and dances and plays, and spends its season in merriment. Manhood labors and endures and acquires, and climbs to the middle summit. Age sighs and trembles and halts, and fails in the closing hours. Then the first volume of history may be sealed, but not forever. The covered grave itself has no promise; it has no inspired revelation; but heaven has both, and bestows them. We could not deny the eternity of death but that Revelation denies it, GOD denies it. With GOD in Revelation then, as our guide, let us consider

GOD'S FAMILY UPON ITS ENTRANCE TO DEATH.

1. *Its physical causes.*

These are disease, exhaustion, weariness, care, sorrow, age, until the house is no longer habitable. Its roof leaks, its walls are shattered, its doors unhinged, its windows open, its partitions gaping and spreading, its fountains stopped, its foundations worm-eaten, its furniture broken and its whole surface moss-covered and weather beaten. The earthly tabernacle is now closed for repairs and the soul moves out.

2. *Its moral causes.*

These are sin. Sin is in the head, sin in the heart, sin in the body and the soul. A change must be wrought, a penalty must be endured. The soul may be pure, but the body must be sifted and shapen anew in incorruption. A law must be vindicated. A solemn silence must precede before the Judge speak and the change come. After that, DEITY will be satisfied, the law content and man glorified.

3. *Its Physical signs.*

These are paleness, coldness, quietness. The feet and hands, no longer obedient, hang in cold horror to the trunk; the viscid clam of the death-angel moistens the brow. As the cables and hawsers of the departing ship are now taken on board, so now the goodly nerves are hauled in from the eye, leaving it in darkness; from the ear, leaving it unconcious; from the taste, so that sweet and bitter are known no more; from the touch, so that the external world, the shore of our mortality, beats and surges unconsciously to the goodly soul.

The blood fountains are less and less forcible until the pulsation of the wrist is silent, and weaker is the dilatation until the heart lapses into stillness. The crimson current has returned to flow out no more.

The lungs hasten to complete *their* task. Frequent and labored are their inspirations, measured to the last are the expirations. All breathings have come and gone but the final one, and the solemn, lingering soul, like a departing pilgrim, takes a last look within the old deserted mansion. It turns to the threshold, raises the latch, opens the door, shuts it and passes out in that final breath. Death pockets the key awhile and walks solemnly away to other engagements, while the spirit, unembarrassed can keep an even flight with the waiting convoys.

The open eye is left fixed and gazing, as if peering wishfully through the window shutters, toward some distant immortal goal after the companion spirit. The awful silence begins. It is the sleep of death.

"Earth to earth and dust to dust!
Here the evil and the just,
Here the youthful and the old,
Here the fearful and the bold,
Here the matron and the maid,
In one silent bed are laid;
Here the vassal and the king,

Side by side lie withering;
Here the sword and scepter rust:
Earth to earth and dust to dust."

4. *The dread of these symptoms.*

These pains and struggles, this coldness and creeping unconsciousness are terrible. Those coffins and whited cerements, this dust and corruption are alarming. All this beauty of form is to be wasted. All these good-byes of kindred souls, this weeping of friends, this sundering of ties, this yielding of fortune, this extradition of claim in reversion to the giver, the exchange from the light of day and the physical glory of this world to darkness, this renunciation of the busy arena of nations, the stirring triumphs of genius, the restless whirl of activity, the loving circles of society and the farewells of all, are heart-rending. This strange prospect of being forgotten by the friends and neighbors we have loved, with no knowledge or wisdom or device in the narrow house is appalling. The certainty that we return no more finishes the picture of sorrow.

(*a*) To the dread of the sinner without hope in his death, is added the certainty that he meets an angry GOD, that he can never enter heaven, that he must sink in darkness forever. O horror of horrors! to have the death of the body supplemented with the death of the soul!

> "O wretched state of dark despair
> To see my GOD remove,
> And fix my doleful station where
> I cannot taste his love."

(*b*) In the Christian, GOD'S child, full of hope, the dread is either reduced or dissipated wholly by the blessed certainiy of future joy and immortality. Take this problem: Given the minuend of dread of death and the subtrahend of eternal life in CHRIST, and what is the remainder? Answer: The dread and terror and sting are a minus quantity. The joy overwhelms the sorrow, so that one says "Thanks be to GOD that giveth us the victory." Another says "I am sweeping through the gates, washed in the blood of the lamb."

5. *The two-fold nature effected by death.*

There is in man a soul as well as a body. The word of GOD reveals it and consciousness affirms it. The body emanated from a divine command just like plants or prowling beasts, from red earth. The body is comely, but weak, weaker than any life of equal size. It is complex, but less protected than any other creature. With only body and animal life, he must die in utter helplessness. But lo! DEITY passes by. He stoops and breathes into the animal man an inspiration. This breath was the generation of soul. This moment soul was incarnated and flesh was made immortal. When soul entered, it brought in passions, affections, memory, imaginations, thought, reason, GOD-like will and conscience.

Grass and animals are the offspring of commands, but Spirit is a likeness or image of GOD. Material body was insignificant, and measured by ounces and pounds, but soul was estimated by comparison with the ALMIGHTY. The marriage of soul and body was consummated and made stronger than death. Soul was not generated from matter as Huxley preaches, but its substance is invisible and intangible. The eyes and ears, the taste and touch which guide to the comprehension of all else around us, are useless in analyzing the mystery of soul. Not even the germ of soul is discoverable; but that it is a distinct entity your consciousness affirms; the phenomena which we see surely moving others, is our second objective witness, and Bible declaration is our third evidence of soul entity.

What this soul is, we cannot know while it mingles with flesh. But that it is distinct and independent of body, is certain. It may come or go, rise or fall, laugh or weep, think or rest, but can never die. How it weaves into and embraces the mortal, in the union of body and spirit, we may not comprehend; it is mystery. So is it mystery that ideas wed a breath of air, as in spoken words, or breathe on metallic type as in books. It is mystery how lightning leaves the clouds and crosses the seas on submerged cables; it is mystery, how heat enters fuel and bears it off into invisibility.

The necessity for the union of soul and body, in the divine plan, is the *apology* for the mystery but not the *explanation* of it. Without body the soul could not enjoy this goodly footstool of God, its air, its food, its beauty, its light, its congenial seasons, its starry canopy. Without soul, the body could not know truth, nor exercise charity, nor fraternize with angels, nor resemble God, nor inherit immortality. With soul and body united, the unity inherits all things and finds a Fatherhood in God. The soul cannot clamor against the body as a weight of corruption, nor the body recoil from the soul as a frightful ghost. Whether in harmony or discord, they must inhabit and inherit together.

6. *The soul and body independent of each other.* Humanity prospects in two directions. Beneath are animals, worms, dust, and *with* them the body affiliates in its materialism; above are angels and GOD, and *to* them the soul is related in all its similitudes. The organic part takes its form, under GOD'S fixed law by vital connection with soul. Rocks are not thus susceptible of organic formation. Around this soul rallies particle after particle to the formation of body. No wonder materialism would invent the monad of Leibnitz, and the protoplasm of Huxley, such is the power of soul to invite organism; such are the rank, fertile weeds of thought when error is the seed. Remove soul and organisn would become dust and ashes.

(*a*) Chemistry and the microscope demonstrate that the protoplasm of Huxley and the monad of Leibnitz are resolvable into primal elements as lifeless as the ashes of the urn. It is analogical and consistent with nature, that an organized human body, deserted by its spirit, must pass into dissolution, assuming new forms, as a chemical compound.

(*b*) Opposed to the revelation and consciousness of the soul's independence, is the formula of the materialist, that *soul is a phenomenon of body or its modification.* Now, body is carbonic acid, water, magnesium, and many other elements. If soul be a modification of body, it must be composed, like body, of carbonic acid and water. And the union of soul and body would be simply the union of *two* parts of Carbonic acid and water instead of *one.* This would be only a change in quantity, not in quality. The whole theory is absurd.

(*c*) Again, soul has a commanding power over body. To obey and gratify soul, body will climb mountains, against gravity, traverse seas and foreign lands, in danger, and unrest, and sacrifice, and self-denial. Body will yield up food and clothing to furnish soul with libraries, and music, and æsthetical refinements. If soul were only a modification of body, here then, is a wonder, one quantity of carbonic acid and water yielding supremacy to another! None of the masters of science ever detected such strange results in the laboratory.

(*d*) Sever the limbs from the body, and the soul is not touched in her powers. Starve or sicken the body to the verge of a skeleton, but the soul remains invulnerable. Let the brain be diseased until a large part is a mass of ruin, but the soul is still wrapped in its citadel of power.

(*e*) Nay, more; the body may burn out its vitals with alcohol, or abuse itself with gross licentiousness, but the soul, ashamed of its counterpart body, still stands up conscious of an existence which the body cannot tamper with. These facts all show that soul and body are distinct and independent of each other, and furnish strong presumption that any dissolution of body would leave soul intact and immortal.

7. *The soul is immortal.*

What a sublime and comforting doctrine! God has created in us an undying part! How it leads into a bright universe of prospects! How it kindles up a lighthouse beyond the dark ocean where our dust dissolves! Matter is never annihilated. No one ever dreams, even in his philosophy, that the oxygen he breathes will ever cease to be, or to be oxygen. If matter be not annihilated, no one so false to analogy or natural law, as to claim less for the soul than for eternal matter.

(*a*) The human conscience looks to man's immortality for its final rewards. Were the present mixing of weal and woe promiscuously, to the righteous and to the wicked, a final adjustment of all deserts, then were the conscience within us a falsehood. Whence this "fearful looking for" unless it is prophetical of future existence?

(*b*) Immortality is demanded to fill the unsatisfied of our present lives; for earth *cannot* do it. This life can only be a preface to a wider destiny beyond. Work is unfinished at death. Personal influence here, evidently, only takes its rise. "To be continued" is written in supplement to the last earthly chapter of human life. "Finis" is only chiseled upon the monuments of the rock-bound fossil. But Revelation makes the transit of death's dark night and brings back the blessed certainty from the lips of God "If a man die he *shall* live again." "God is the God of the living." The "house not made with hands" now "To let" certifies immortality.

8. *The philosophy of dying.*

We have seen that soul and body are independent of each other, and that destruction to body is not destruction to soul. We have further discovered that the moral cause of death was sin and that the moral result was to pave the way, through death, for purified immortality to body as well as soul. We are now prepared to understand how the Christian family yields up to death and prefers it. It is hard for youth to die; it is easier for age. How radiant is life to the young! How limpid and fair its outlook! How sweet and tender its emotions! How sparkling and brimful its festivities! These things captivate young life and urge perpetuity.

How different is age! Every modification of existence is a burden; every song a plaintive refrain; every feeling an infirmity; every prospect a dimness; every change a further exhaustion.

While the body is thus failing so that the soul, is out at the elbows, and threadbare at the knees, and gaping from the feet, and uncomfortable in every part, locking itself in the body's inmost chambers, heaping up the fuel when the night chills come on, then how of the soul's preferences? Does it meditate removal? Yes. The treasures laid up beyond become more valued and inviting. Religion turns all embarrassments and longings into hopes of deliverance. The unendurable weight of infirmity drives while the eternal weight of glory draws. The problem comes when earth reveals her first disappointment, thus: "Is it better to depart and be with CHRIST?" The soul thus figures it: "Earth is yet too pleasing, heaven too far away, death too gloomy," and the answer comes: "Not yet." But disappointments encompass and multiply, and infirmities force the old problem: "*Is* it better to depart and be with CHRIST yet?" Again the soul approaches the blackboard of destiny to decipher the problem. Errors are found in the first computation, and the data are modified. Lately the sun was found, by Astronomers, to be nearer than at first supposed; so now, the soul's heaven proves nearer, death less terrible, and the astonishing truth comes at last. As gravitation revealed its secret to Newton after ten years of reflection, so this conclusion of moral gravity startles and moves the Christian: "It *is* better to depart and be with CHRIST." It *is* better to join the family in heaven. It *is* better to wear a crown of glory than a crown of thorns. It *is* better to dwell at home, in a mansion near the palace of the universe, than to tarry longer on the very rim of darkness. It *is* better to retreat from the indefensible fortress of mortality and make a firm stand forever in the high, impregnable citadel of immortality. "To die is gain."

When death comes God matures even the young Christian to the same desires and preferences. Crucifying pains, racking diseases, burning fevers and bitter disappointments may ripen the young spirit as early frost ripens the summer fruit. Thus the philosophy of dying daily is to disarm the final shock and mature the Christian to prefer and welcome the inevitable *finálē.* When the darkness comes, we know a little four year old child who always says: "Mamma it is so dark, I'm afraid; put me to sleep; I'm afraid of the dark, mamma." So the soul reaches this cry to God: "Put me to sleep in Jesus, I am afraid of the darkness of this world's valley and shadow."

9. *Man's extremity, God's opportunity.* The preparation in the land of mansions for a Christian's death is quite different from the earthly preparation. Behold man afflicted, tormented, distressed, praying for deliverance, panting to go hence. This is the opportunity of God. This warfare in probation bruises the Christian soldier. A discharge is written by the Angel of life, signed and officially sealed by the Blessed God, and passed over to the angel of death. Deity orders and death obeys, thus: "Death, do you see my suffering servant in yon-

der lower world?" "Yes," says Death, solemnly. "Do you see how he is oppressed with pain?" "Yes." "Do you see how he is groaning for deliverance?" "Yes," answers Death. "It is enough," says the pitying GOD. "Let him come up higher—Let him come to ME—Go, Death, and relieve him—Take with you a good legion of my swiftest messengers—Relieve and dismiss the Spirit and send it home with the Angels—It will only beautify it to be separated thus—Whisper a consolation to the body before you put it to sleep—Tell it of the Resurrection—Then breathe a gentle stillness and peace around it, close its eyes and let it slumber—Then come away, Death, let it alone, your work is done, when the body sleeps. Kind friends will consign it to the peaceful tomb—But it matters not, I will come again, by and by, and bring it to myself—It is no difference, Death, if you let the body fall into the sea, or consume by fire, or bleach on battle fields—I will guard the dust and fashion it over better than now into a glorious form. I will issue to my servant Gabriel, the *Habeas Corpus* of the Resurrection in the fullness of time." GOD ends his commands, and swift as the light of a star, the death Angel and the bright legion who return the soul to God, pass heaven's mid-light and reach the dying saint. "Precious in the sight of the Lord is the death of His saints." Now the death-angel, divinely commissioned, solemnly, mournfully, tenderly begins the task. He feels for the ligaments and cords that bind soul and body. Here he cuts a thread, there he gently breaks a tie, and yonder he loosens a bond. There is only time for an address of welcome, "Welcome death," and a last good-bye, and a hallelujah of triumph. And now death gently feels for the strings of the heart. Cautiously they are severed by the experienced angel. The separation is effected. The consecrated cross drops just as the struggle is over. The work is done Instantly the soul starts with the Blessed legions. The body sleeps silently, sadly, sweetly. You remember when mother slept the last sleep, how sweetly she rested from her labors; the countenance was relaxed from care; it was blessed slumber. When father died, his hands had reached toward heaven in prayer for deliverance, and they fell relaxed as the prayer was answered, and the angels let his body sleep. His works do follow him. They live on like his soul. The Christian's death is not an accident, but heaven-ordered.

"There is weeping on earth for the lost!
  There is bowing in grief to the ground!
But rejoicing and praise 'mid the sanctified host,
  For a Spirit in Paradise found!
Though brightness hath passed from the earth,
  Yet a star is new-born in the sky,
And a soul hath gone home to the land of its birth!
  Where are pleasures and fullness of joy!
And a new harp is strung and a new song is given
  To the breezes that float o'er the gardens of heaven."

10. *Dying testimony a proof of man's entrance upon immediate immortality.* Of the Progenitor of man it is recorded, "And all the days that Adam lived were nine hundred and thirty years and he died." Similar is the only record of Seth, Enos, Canaan, Mahalaleel, Jared, Methuselah, Lamech and Noah. Of one the sublime record is; "Enoch walked with God, and he was not, for God took him." The patriarch of faith, "Abraham, gave up the ghost, and died in an old age, an old man, and full of years, and was gathered to his people." Not the bodies of his people in the cave Machpelah; the word "people" is masculine, "to his fathers," and they were buried in Chaldea, not in Canaan. It was soul that was gathered into heaven, among faithful souls. A similar record is made of Ishmael,

Isaac, Jacob and Aaron. This is the obituary of the Psalmist: "So David slept with his fathers and was buried in the city of David." Another man of GOD has this notice: "Elijah went up by a whirlwind into heaven." The man of patient affliction is thus dismissed: "So Job died, being old and full of days." The final words of the blessed LORD before death were these: "Father into thy hand I commend my spirit." St. Stephen bowing to receive death said: "LORD JESUS receive my spirit." Paul said: "The time of my departure is at hand. I have fought a good fight, I have finished my course, I have kept the faith. Henceforth there is laid up for me a crown of righteousness." The great Webster whispered back: "I still live." Payson said: "The celestial city is full in view; its glories beam upon me; its breezes fan me; its odors are wafted to me; its music strikes upon my ear, and its spirit breathes into my heart."

And whether words are recorded or not, this is the sum total of the entire family of GOD in the consummation of the dying hour: "Blessed are the dead which die in the Lord from henceforth: Yea, saith the Spirit, that they may rest from their labors, and their works do follow them."

The CHRIST is not to day in the new tomb of Joseph of Arimathea. The real Isaac and Jacob are not in the cave of Machpelah. Was it Abel's soul that was slain? Is Moses dead and buried in the valley of Moab? No; he has been seen, all glorious, since that day, on the mount of transfiguration. Is the real Abraham asleep with his fathers in Machpelah's lonely cave? No; he is known, and has been seen since in Heaven as "Father Abraham." Are Gideon, and Barak, and Sampson, and Jephthah, and Samuel all mouldering in the soil of Judea? Is Wickliffe floating in his burned ashes, which were sifted into the sea? Is Paul under the sod of Italy? Are Wesley and Clark and Bunyan in the church-yards of England? Is Washington in the urn of Mount Vernon? Is Bishop Baker annihilated under the snows of Concord! Is Bishop Kingsley indeed crumbling where he fell in Palestine? Are Bishops Thomson and Clark forever gone in the valleys of the west? "Our Fathers, where are they?" Are they eternally in the soil? No. Blessed be GOD. "These all died in the faith," and "the faith" has triumphantly exalted the free and better portion to glory.

Though the Rocky Mountains flee away, the

Alps sink down in dissolving fires, and the stars cease to gleam in beauty and sadness from the sky, yet all God's Family, who enter the valley and shadow of death, shall sleep well, and in the eternal day awake to immortality, and shine like the brightness of stars forever and ever.

CHAPTER III.

God's Family asleep, or The Intermediate State.

WE have ascertained how the *Family of God* were put to sleep in death. We have left their bodies in the darkness and stillness of the grave. There, to them, ages pass. The very mound of earth, their only monument, sinks down to surface levels. The obelisk of marble finally crumbles, and yet we hear no revelation from the grave. Winter's snow and summer's sun succeed each other. Generation after generation falls down in the chambers of death, and the city of slumber outnumbers all the cities of earth. Within its solemn shrine bone falls from its bone, ligaments relax, flesh is disintegrated from flesh and skin dissolves into traceless ashes. It is the solemn execution of that sweeping proclamation, "Dust thou art and unto dust shalt thou return."

"Death's harvests of a thousand years
  Have here been gathered in,
The vintage where the wine was tears
  The laborer was sin;
The loftiest passions and the least
  Lie sleeping side by side,
And love hath reared its staff of rest
  Beside the grave of pride."

The long funeral processions of weeping friends slowly move home again from the cemeteries of earth where loved ones are buried, and they cry "Dead! dead!! dead!!!" Glad devils, too, attend all the funerals of earth, and behold the cold, narrow tomb, and the triumph of death, and they swoop, like chimney swallows down, down the caverns and vaults and chimneys of perdition, grimly chanting, "Dead! dead!! dead!!!" Guardian angels behold the bodies put into the tomb, and return sadly home to glory saying "Dead! dead!! dead!!!"

Ages upon ages roll by, the tomb itself is leveled and lost, and angels, devils and men solemnly testify "Dead! dead!! dead!!!"

But let us rise above this mute slumber of body and seek the soul. If we were "Such stuff as dreams are made off, and our little life * * * rounded with a sleep," the Intermediate State lengthens out unto an eternal sleep whose darkness is triumphant. But if the soul live on, above "the wreck of matter," as we learned in the last chapter, there arises the question whether there is not a state just subsequent to death, extending to judgment, when soul and body are less united, glorious and happy, than in the re-union of the resurrection. Such state, antecedent to resurrection, or Intermediate State, does exist and it is worthy of special consideration.

To the Bible we go. Let us light up this Lamp to our feet and light to our pathway. It casts a beam of light across the dark valley and shadow, and makes a revelation of that half way house to immortality. Such is the only possible inference of passages pointing to the resurrection.

1. *The Intermediate State different from the Resurrection.* CHRIST says, (John 5 & 28) "The hour is coming, in the which all that are in the graves shall hear his voice and shall come forth." Isaiah says, (26 & 15) "Thy dead men shall live, together with my dead body shall they arise." So Paul breaks the mystery of the resurrection. (1 Cor. 15 & 52.) "For the trumpet shall sound, and the dead

shall be raised incorruptible and we shall be changed." Again, he breathes from GOD consolation concerning the ones fallen asleep. "For the Lord himself shall descend from heaven with a shout, with the voice of the Arch-angel and with the trump of GOD; and the dead in CHRIST shall rise first. All these and other texts, pre-suppose a mighty change to which the Intermediate State must be a previous condition.

2. *The Intermediate state is not equivalent to final Judgment.* The works that do follow the dead spread out in diverging lines, affecting the generations to the end of time. Responsible influence is going on, and rising up into a power, moving the Church, the nation and the world, long after the body dies. Influence cannot be final and sealed to a man, until the whole human family meet with its GOD, in the last day, and the value of the souls, moved to salvation or destruction by each man can be estimated by the Judge. Hence neither the righteous nor the wicked, can at death, enter upon the fullness of their eternal state, until their works can run the whole probation of time. The departed soul, therefore, awaits *in part*, its full joy or misery until the Resurrection. For though, to the

good, it is certain at death that their Spirits are washed, and to the wicked that they can never be transformed to purity, yet the degree of good and evil is not yet meted out; and the height of enjoyment or the depth of misery cannot yet be realized. Intermediate influence set to work in life, may change the quantity but never the quality of the future reward. The star crowns cannot all be counted at death, nor the Spirits lost forever, by one's instrumentality. The trophies are not, even to-day, counted up of a meek Moses, a faithful Abraham, a weeping Jeremiah, a loving John, a crucified JESUS, a believing Paul, a sacrificing Luther, or an emancipating Lincoln. So the wages of sin are not yet all enumerated in the mighty columns of Nero, or Ahab, or Pilate, or Paine, or Darwin, or Satan.

3. *Errors must be repelled concerning the Intermediate State.* We diverge to repel some of the untheological and silly opinions crept into some hearts and derived inadvertently from heathen sources.

(*a*) Before the New Testament light, the Hebrew, *Sheal* and the Greek *Hades* was by unscriptural theories, made a confused land of Spirits. It was located beneath us, a dreamy, dark, moping, wandering, ghostly chasm which souls promiscuously entered at death. Earth-pressed mortals sought this land, as it brought into a common twilight all the separated of time.

(*b*) Another error: that dismissed Spirits stay in the vicinity of the body. Hence haunted houses, ghostly churchyards, careless demons and spirit-rapping disembodied simpletons. The great gulf which separates the righteous from the wicked may not again be overpassed on this middle world. Graver employments detain the departed, infinitely graver than earth can yield. No mortal need hope or fear that Spirits will loiter around under chairs, tables, beds, in clocks, closets and among mantle-piece ornaments, as if they were out of employment until the judgment day.

(*c*) Still another mistake has been insisted upon; that souls leaving the dying body, seek a homestead in some other living form. Such a theory is worthy the taste of those evil Spirits which, when cast out, besought that they might enter into a herd of swine. Yet the swine body and the evil Spirits were not adapted to each other, as the stampede and drowning in Galilee fully demonstrated.

Bodies, like garments, must be made to order, or an untidy, sack-like, wrinkled fullness would occur. As much expect a swine-coat to be an appropriate habitation for a man, and a mansion with parlors, pictures and libraries, would be suitable for a swine, as, that an exchange of bodies would make a good fit, or satisfy the living principle. This theory is old, and, though exploded, it bubbles up from some infernal deep, ready for another explosion. It was called the transmigration of souls. So Pythagoras believed and taught. So the Egyptian philosophy published, that the departed, after passing through the form of every bird and beast during about three thousand years, could enter a human body again. The monadic biology of Huxley and the development hypothesis of Darwin are only modifications and plagiarisms of this transmigration theory of Plato, Pythagoras, and many oriental philosophers.

(*d*) The next error is the theory that soul sleeps with body in one deep, dark ocean of death. They say the Intermediate State is a soul sleep as well as a body sleep. This is unscriptural and obnoxious to the contemplation of a deathless Spirit. The grave is gloomy enough in bodily dissolution without unscripturally heaping its clods of forgetfulness upon the soul also.

To our lamp we go again. "Light the lamp" we cry in our darkness. CHRIST says: "Whosoever believeth on me shall never die." And again, "This day shalt thou be with me in Paradise." Paul seals up the certainty of life. "It is better to depart and be with CHRIST."

(*e*) The next error we name is "That there is a purgatory, or middle state; and that the souls of imperfect Christians, therein detained, are helped by the prayers of the faithful." This is a Roman Catholic doctrine. It resolves all persons, at or after death, into three classes, good, bad and indifferent. The indifferent class of souls is the portion in question. It asserts that souls too good apparently to be damned and too bad to be saved, are suspended, after death, in a middle estate of probation, a place called purgatory from which they may be purchased by money or human merit, or prayed out by living friends. But the Bible shows the only true purgatory, holds closed doors and none may enter except on business. But, like the parlor, web and other phenomena about the cunning spider is this place; for those who enter purgatory on business "Ne'er come out again," to report to the living. May as well attempt to bribe the spider with gold or move him with prayers and tears to release the "silly fly," as to expect that gold is current coin in eternity, and will buy off a soul partly bad from the clutches of the evil one, when death has fixed its destiny. No prayer of CHRIST, or Moses, or the Prophets, or any inspired person was ever recorded for the dead. Every Bible prayer was limited to the living. No Bible intimation is any-where made of the remotest possibility of changing the state of the dead. It was only a monkish device to rob the mourners of money: it has no Scriptural apology, and can only be based upon and sustained by superstition.

4. *The soul's intermediate place of rest.* It is *somewhere.* It is not necessary nor Scriptural that the soul, at death, pass through moral gradations, or Gehenna, or Hades, or Tartarus, or Paradise, or Purgatory. But straight as an arrow and swift as a beam of light, we fly to JESUS in death. The soul's place therefore is the same as that of its eternal rest. To put on full immortality, to achieve final triumph, the resurrection body is essential. Let St. Stephen sublimate his soul in faith, breath-

ed of the HOLY GHOST as he cries in death, "LORD JESUS receive my spirit." Let JESUS himself remove the veil to the pardoned thief, "This day shalt thou be with me in Paradise." Let the great apostle Paul, "be absent from the body," then is he "present with the LORD."

5. *This middle state is one of perfect living powers.* On the Mount of Transfiguration, two saints, centuries old in spirit-land experience, met and talked familiarly with the LORD. To Elijah it was then a glorious theme how the missionary should carry the consecrated cross all over the earth in triumph, and to Moses how the Spiritual Israel would finally reach the heavenly Canaan. Moses and Elias were creatures of bright, powerful consciousness at that interview, and rational and full of such bliss and knowledge as a residence of fifteen hundred years in heaven might give.

The rich man died and lifted up his eyes in hell. Also Lazarus escaped to heaven and nestled in the bosom of Abraham. In the solemn dialogue which ensued, they were all three conscious, the rich man full of prayer and anxiety for the living and torment for himself, Abraham and Lazarus full of bliss, and holiness, and immortality.

John was about to worship the messenger on Patmos, but was arrested by the clear, conscious announcement, "I am of thy brethren the prophets." That same Patmos vision culminated in the blessed discovery of one of the hiding places of the soul in its intermediate state. For when the fifth seal was opened John saw under the altar the martyred host who cried, "O Lord how long?" They had white robes and were to rest a little for the incoming martyrs of all time.

All these characters were conscious, and, save the one who lifted up his eyes in hell, were happy beyond earthly life. This consciousness was not questioned nor discussed by any cotemporary. It was the faith of the Church. These examples become to us the sureties of the existence of GOD's entire family in happy consciousness in the Intermediate state. The doctrine reveals the glorious enjoyment that meets the righteous when he dies. It kindles hope and joy in the heart of the departing, knowing that no fear of annihilation can distrust immortality, but that in many respects they rise to blessed enjoyments in the home circle of the heavenly.

6. *Shall we know each other there?*

Soul has its peculiar traits, qualities, phenomena and motions which combined constitute personal identity. It has not flesh, but it still has form. Instead of the five senses which body possesses it may have more than equivalent methods of communication. The death of body is not the death of ability ; the death of the eye does not blind the soul, nor that of the ear make it deaf. New and multiplied and infinitely varied avenues may be opened at death in the soul to acquaint it with surroundings and kindred. This doubtless is the Scriptural view. Thus Lazarus and Abraham were recognized in heaven. Thus Samuel was identified. The soul is not therefore a floating, formless mass of gas, like a chaotic nebula of unformed worlds in the sky; it is not a chameleon cloud, changing with the breeze and the heat. But it doubtless has a well-known form, a perfect spiritual body. The view of soul having fixed traits, will sufficiently account for the recognition, even among spirits, before the resurrection of the just. Such recognition is revealed to the living in the Word. And it is the dear solace to the bereaved, when parent, child, companion have departed; for in the "sweet by and by," a blessed re-union is anticipated. This is the Spirit of God, the Holy Comforter making a direct confirmation to the spirit of man, of future re-union and eternal friendship. It is the function of memory to embalm and retain forever. Memory is as deathless as the soul. All the bliss of heaven would be marred by making it a world of strange ghosts which cannot communicate former history, or trial, or victory to old companions who have similarly lived and died. Spirits of heaven are no less wise and penetrating than spirits of earth. There we shall see face to face. We shall know as we are known.

"Over the river they beckon to me,
Loved ones who've crossed to the further side;
The gleam of their snowy robes I see,
But their voices are lost in the dashing tide."

Affection begun on earth is as eternal as the beautiful soul which kindles its flame below. It is only a cosmological change not a psychological.

"Bright in that happy land
Beams every eye.
Kept by a Father's hand
Love cannot die."

Without heavenly recognition the poet is wrong

and love *must* die. But to know each other will feed its holy flame forever.

There are misunderstandings on earth where love only intended blessings. Time and earth furnish no opportunity for explanations, eternity and heaven must. They will, therefore furnish recognition as the first means for the solution of such mysterious conduct of friends. Am I to be an eternal pilgrim and stranger on the other shore? No! No! Is my child, or my student to be treated with stern discipline here, in love, which cannot well be explained nor comprehended, and may I not in the heavenly world make the explanation? Doubtless I may recognize these children of earth and explain in the brighter light of heaven. The reason, why strange bereavements and afflictions, have superannuated and clouded the years of my friend's life can only be explained by my friend in the light of eternity. There could be no consciousness, no memory, no perception, no personal identity in heaven unless we first know self, and then "know as we are known." There is necessity for this recognition to explain how individual toil, sacrifice, works, holiness and suffering can be made known, as the Scriptures affirm, in the judgment day.

Every man will be made known in that day, and his shining there will correspond to his righteousness here.

A dear boy has been stolen from his parents by Indians. The young parents go mourning for their first born until infirmity bends them and time has snowed upon their heads. They pass fifty years alone in the cabin, and a stranger in life's prime calls at the door of the aged pair. Out of a half century's bereavement the mother says "That is our-long lost child; it is his smile and his voice." The father says "It must be his eyes, and forehead, and cheek, and chin, and walk." The former boy is now changed from the white head of infancy to the gray head of age; time has carried him on from three to fifty three, but yet a father and mother recognize him in all the changes. This is earthly recognition. And so mother, father, son, daughter, wife, husband, brother, sister, neighbor, frien^d^ become familiar again on the other shore. JESU may elicit the chief attention of the redeemed for ever. Grave, grand, glorious works and ways c GOD may be the theme of perpetual investigatioı but the Bible clearly sets forth that we shall kno\ as we are known.

7. *Death does not change the soul's, nature but only its place.*

The decree is "He that is unjust, let him be unjust still; and he that is filthy let him be filthy still; and he that is righteous let him be righteous still; and he that is holy let him be holy still." The chief change is on body, in the transfer from cold, frigid earth to balmy heaven; from the arctic clay-clogs and fleshly wrappings of winter to the white robes of perennial summer. True, the soul may breathe new atmosphere and be mightily strengthened. It may press down cups of bliss that run over forever. Eternal health, beyond fear, may dissipate all sadness far away. Angel guides and teachers may conduct from the centre to the circumference of heaven and fill with beautiful knowledge. Friendships and affections re-united forever may firmly knit us into the holy brotherhood of saint and angel, and all these glories united may push our souls up nearer GOD, and bid them shine like the stars, yet the moral capital is that which is gathered into the soul's treasury before death. The quantity of moral power and purity may be infinitely increased and expanded, but the quality is unchanged by death.

"There no shadow shall bewilder,
There life's vain parade is o'er;
There the sleep of sin is broken,
And the dreamer dreams no more."

8. *Is there danger of a soul's being overlooked?*

Will the angels be sure to gather every soul, or may not some occasional souls fall in death, and, like the gleaning of the reapers, by accident, be neglected, and wander in the Spirit land without a guide? We reply; GOD knows all, sees all, provides for all. There is no accident with GOD. There is no failure to His love. Not a good soul departs from earth, but the FATHER knows and orders it; not a rail-road train leaps into a deep gorge with its destruction of saint and sinner, but a permissive Providence has a sufficient angel convoy on the fatal spot before the train's arrival to bear the fallen righteous home; there is not a battle-field where thousands fall amid the deadly strife and clash of arms, but legions of heaven, more numerous than the legions of earth, hover around to carry Christian soldiers home to GOD; and from the roar of artillery they suddenly wake to the songs of immortality. Not an epidemic sweeps through the city to reap its harvest of souls, but the angel harvesters bear every sheaf to the garner of GOD. Not a lonely cabin loses its solitary inmate, not a Christian pilgrim is suddenly torn by wild beasts, but the All-seeing Eye is providing for the disembodied soul. Not a ship in ocean's storm is buried under the billows with its cargo of souls, but He who made the deep and rides the storm, commands some chariot of fire from the livery of Heaven, to transport His saints to the land where storms are no more. Never does the angel of death start from the throne with a commission to relieve a soul, but an angel of life, swift as the other, starts with a commission to bring the relieved soul home. Not one soul can, by any possibility, ever be missed. To *fear* it is to doubt the omniscience, the omnipresence, the omnipotence, the goodness, the promise of GOD.

9. *What is the intermediate state of infants?*

A bereaved parent now inquires, who will care for the tender babe's soul and deal with it lovingly as it goes from a mother's arms over the dark river? Who will now meet it and nestle it and soothe it and quiet it in the Spirit land? These are only the tender babes, the little ones, the fair-haired pets, who sought and required a mother's comfort and care. Now that they are torn from the maternal bosom, will they be orphans in heaven? Will they weep there for the presence of a mother? Will they be un-cared for among the strange spirits of glory? Do you know JESUS? It was a time of his poverty. He was treading His familiar rounds in Judea. Weary mothers sought His blessing upon their little ones. What did He do? He stooped, took them in His arms, blessed them, opened the divine heart, uttered from His precious lips a Revelation, sweet, tender, all-sufficient, special. "Suffer the little children to come to *Me*"—not to Moses, nor the prophets, nor the apostles, not by any conditions of repentance or faith, they have not sinned—Let them all come directly to "*Me*, for of such is the kingdom of heaven." All the infants of every people and generation are literally peopling heaven. "Behold," says CHRIST, "their angels are before my Father," nearest Him, most holy and happy and blest. If the REDEEMER's tenderness ever overflowed, if He ever especially revealed a doctrine directly, which the Spirit itself had never disclosed to inspired penman, it was in this gracious interview. It is enough; the promise is ample; the divine heart is astir. And if there be a specialty in the REDEEMER'S work, it is to bring home these sinless children and wipe their tears and introduce them to loving angels. Soon, with loosened tongues, they learn the story of redemption, the language of heaven and the song of Moses and the lamb; soon they excel in knowledge, they are infants no more; they become familiar among the hosts of glory.

How comforting to a bereft parent! How sweet and holy the song of children in Heaven as the first consciousness they ever had dawns there, and they learn from the lips of angels the precious theology that, although they were the seed of a sinful race, yet the blood of the LAMB washed out the stain of original sin, and they were brought home without ever knowing or offending the Creator's laws.

Such is the part of the family circle gathered in Heaven to-day. Such is their Intermediate State revealed in the word of GOD. Such is the Bible promise and prospect of faith that opens out an immediate heaven of love and enjoyment to those who in righteousness have lived, in hope have died, and now fly at GOD'S commands with angel guides, out of the body, out of mortality, out of labor, out of darkness, out of death, into life, into day, into rest, into immortality, into the innumerable company of angels, the Church of the First born, triumphant in their joys. Blessed be GOD for His Revelation of the home of the soul! The martyrs are there.

Meantime we must visit the earthly. We left the body in the ground. Death has not been wholly swallowed up in victory. This dust must come forth; every particle must be rescued; the winds must bring back the dust they carried away; the sea must uncover its hidden dust; the common soil of the cemetery must retreat from the dissolved elements committed to its care; the earthquake that swallowed up cities must open again and disgorge its trust. Revelation has promised it; GOD has said it; the triumph of JESUS over death, hell and the grave requires it; the delighted universe that gazed upon the opening scenes of the tragedy demands it; and our hearts accept it as the most precious doctrine of existence.

We recapitulate the chapter in a few words. What we have stated as doctrine is Bible truth; it is not speculation, but a just interpretation of the Word. We have seen:

1. The Intermediate State is by no means the Resurrection, but from the former to the latter is a vast change.

2. The Intermediate State is not the final judgment.

3. We have repelled several errors about the Intermediate State.

4. We have proven that immediately after death the pious dead are in heaven.

5. We have seen this state is a knowable state and full of consciousness.

6. We have seen that death does not affect the quality of soul.

7. We have certified, by the Word, that the infants of all generations and kindred and climes are ushered into sinless and happy consciousness.

8. We have been assured that no soul will be accidentally omitted.

9. Finally we have concluded from the entire subject that the Intermediate State is to continue until the end of the world, at the general judgment, the awakening of GOD's sleeping family from death.

CHAPTER IV.

God's Family Awakened, or The Resurrection.

WE now come to the fourth scene in this immortal tragedy of the divine family, the resurrection from the dead. The consummation of this mighty problem depends wholly upon the power and will of God. Our faith that He will surely accomplish it, rests upon His Revelation. This is full, ample, and satisfying, yet the infidel, without God and faith, hangs upon our advance at every step, and makes denial of the doctrine. Let us therefore expose infidelity before we advance.

Some infidels who deny the Bible, deny also the resurrection of the dead, on the ground of its absurdity, inexpediency, impossibility, &c. Others who accept the Bible, or portions of it, with their interpretations, attempt to modify or destroy that part which teaches a resurrection of the dying body.

On these questions the full-blooded infidels, and the semi infidels agree and may be treated together.

1. Some Infidel of literal resurrection, a Cannibal of the resurrection, brings this obstacle: The body changes its particles in about seven years; and if resurrected, which septennial body shall be taken? Is it the infant body, the mature body, or the dying body? The question itself is not important. It is merely dust upon the eye of the infidel, which comes from his wallowing in the darkness and the mire. Yet we reply: God could raise either or all, but the Scriptures signify with clearness, that He will raise the dying body, the one which the soul left. This is the only one which died; this is the only one which must be grasped triumphantly from death. Personal identity is continued at any time of life, in the particular body which is then the soul's home. Any other doctrine would make us irresponsible for any acts committed seven years ago, on the plea that the body of new particles is not responsible for the former body's deeds. This would debar from imprisonments, which lasted beyond seven years, or from capital punishments unless executed within seven years of the crime; it would cause us to lose the rewards of

actions seven years after their committal: it would require all marriages and other sacred contracts, like vaccination to be either void or repeated every seven years; it would supercede divorce laws, since all who might be dissatisfied in conjugal bonds, could, if patient seven years, go out in a perpetual jubilee; indeed, by such theory, our life would be as many distinct persons as our age is divisible by seven. Such doctrine is absurd. Personal identity is unchanged amid all changes. The gold of the mine, imbedded in gross granite, is the gold of the purifying fire and the gold of the future dollar, but how gloriously changed and fashioned and having the King's image and superscription upon it.

2. Here is vegetable infidelity. It says: The dead body dissolves to dust and gases and enters new living forms which other humanity eats; at other times it is devoured by the cannibal, and he in turn is eaten by other cannibals, and the particles are thus caused to belong to many persons at their death, making a resurrection of identical particles impossible. Yet "With God all things are possible." Revelation does not specifically refer to cannibalism, but faith takes God's omnipotence and fully interprets the general promises upon the

subject, into a satisfactory solution. God can command particles thus appropriated once, by some law, well known to Him, but unknown to us, to absolutely reject, ever after, any combination or assimilation into a second body. He who promises the resurrection can easily follow every particle, precious in the body of a dying saint, and guard it against any permanent union with other human body. The identical body when raised is to be glorified, refashioned, reformed, crystalized, so to speak, into an immortal form. Those parts which perpetuate the individual by food in digestion, and those parts which perpetuate the species by generation, are not essential in the new state of existence, and their particles may, or may not be a part of the glorified body; God knows. Much of our present bulk is temporary, extraneous and circumstantial to our present condition. The resurrection, we think, contemplates the rejection of these, just as the shroud, the winding sheet, and other funeral cerements are rejected. As Kingsley remarks, cannibals do not eat the bones, nor the skin, nor many other portions. When cannibalism occurs it is not the every day diet, but the occasional feast of long intervals. Naturally but a small part of the devoured would become a part of the devourer. And but a small part of the decayed body enters the vegetable world so as to be taken incidentally as food in civilized lands. Even all this by command of GOD, may go to the temporary parts of the system. These are only suggestions of the expediency of GOD. But our true answer to this infidel cavil is of greater certainty and higher authority, viz: that the entire process of the resurrection is miraculous and based upon the attributes of GOD. He could so order the particles of the resurrection body to be miraculously sacred, though they pass through the digestion of the cannibal, or float through vegetation, or be carried by the winds or waters, in a thousand circuitous routes, that they reject all union, sacred forever to the appropriated dust of the dying. Since it is all a miracle of GOD, He may in ten thousand ways, inconceivable to us, guard the dust and fulfill His word and promise to the letter. The objection makes a flat denial of GOD's word and GOD's ability; we come back to the Word and accept both. So you might deny many of the sublime facts of Astronomy, Chemistry, and other sciences, which experiment and demonstration prove. The whole subject must be carried back to the Word as a miracle. Go to GOD's power. He can do all things.

3. Next is the dyspeptic infidel. He says: "The raising of the dying body would bring the most ghastly form we ever possessed, the infant in its frailty, the old man in his wrinkled decrepitude, and the wasted skeleton of the sick bed." We reply; You lean on natural laws again, and deny the Word. The glorious reforming of these particles with the exclusion of every deformity and the inspiration of eternal life and eternal vigor, and the image made like unto the glorious body of the LORD, will make an evenness and general uniformity, not very unlike in all saints. We say to that friend recovered from disease, "You appear better than I ever saw you before;" and we may say in the resurrection to our parents who died in infirmity, and our infants who perished in helplessness: "You appear infinitely more glorious and lovely than I ever saw you before." We shall be changed not in matter, but in form; as the silver ore is changed to vessels of beauty and honor, as the carbon is changed to the diamond, as the soil and moisture and floating carbon are changed to the grains and fruits, so that which was

sown in corruption shall be raised in incorruption.

4. Next is the chronic infidel. Says he: "The body is matter, gross, unspiritual, unworthy of immortality, subject to infirmity." But not so. Rocks are not subject to infirmity; gold and silver do not rust; diamonds, pearls, jaspers, chalcedonies, sapphires, emeralds and beryls are not subject to disease. Age only polishes them; matter is not sinful, nor subject to sin, but spirit is.

5. Next we meet the croaking infidel. He avers; "The body weighs down the soul by gravity to earth; it is a prison, a hindrance, a clog of clay, unworthy of the soul, a thing from which we may seek riddance." To this we answer; The body, immortal as well as the soul, will be changed. The soul will be enlarged, strengthened, honored, obeyed; the body so fashioned and glorified that it will be a glorious union of counterparts. The nature will not be as here, flesh and blood in grossly commanding moods, but flesh and blood so re-fashioned that spirit has the ascendency, and hence the union will be rather spiritual than carnal. The gravity or weight of matter in the glorified body may be countermanded! GOD can very readily order that gravity never affect it nor the contact

of wind, water or solid, as they affect ordinary matter.

Let us seek common illustrations from nature to assist our faith. Chlorate of Potassa, a solid, when heated in the retort turns to Oxygen, a body invisible, light, penetrating, strong, ardent, pure, elastic, never returning back again to chlorate of potassa.

Again; observe a small insect, with strong light, under the microscope, and it is transparent as glass, pierced through and through with lines of light. So God can, and will speak these bodies of ours into forms so glorious as to be transparent to each other, invisible to the natural eye of this world, imponderable to the attractions of matter, freed forever and perfectly by His higher law of miracle, from all the effects of ordinary contact with gross matter in this world.

6. The Gnostics and Marcionites denied the resurrection because they thought matter itself sinful, and that eternal deliverance from it was the greatest blessing. St. Paul, in Corinthians, was addressing some Gnostics who were in the Church. His Greek word "*Pos*," translated *how*, refers to the possibility of the resurrection and

not to the manner. Paul by the illustration of the wheat, flesh and celestial bodies, only refers to this possibility amid such denials. The second question, " with what body do they come forth?" is simply the Corinthian denial that any conceivable body, known to the existing theories of philosophy could possibly be joined to soul, without detriment.

7. Paul points us to the sun. The sun is a glorious body, a celestial body, but the spectroscope has recently revealed it to have the same matter as the earth. The stars are very glorious, but they, too, reveal their identity of elements by the same instrument. The apostle wholly omits the actual mode God uses in the resurrection; it was not the *question* which troubled the Corinthians, but the *fact*. It is clear however that Paul does speak of the body, the well known form called the human body, and makes it a miracle of God, beyond our comprehension, that we shall be changed.

8. Some Jewish Rabbis contended for an indestructible germ called *Luz* in their language, from which the whole body grew like a plant from a seed. Justin Martyr, who as a cotemporary knew the spirit of their argument, replies, "If the body

be not raised complete, it would argue want of power in God." Maimonedes says, "Nothing can be properly called a resurrection, but the very same soul in the very same body." This germ theory is clearly outside of any scriptural interpretations; it is human invention. It is not a resurrection at all, but a vegetation, or a new creation from a particle.

9. All scientific objections and methods which explode the resurrection, are human attempts to bring down the divine mysteries to human comprehension, and reconcile them with human philosophies. Such scientists say *nothing* is possible with God, except it agree with science. They shut their eyes in reading Revelation, but widely open them in reading philosophy. "If immortals," say they, "have bodies, eating is essential," yet in a human sense, God's immortals need not eat. Woe to religion when science insists on dictating the interpretations of the Bible! Science is the Hand-maid of Religion, not her Goddess,

In the transfiguration, the face of Christ shone as the sun and his raiment was white as snow. This is man's immortal model. In this world spirit serves body, but there, body shall be more like and serve spirit; it becomes spiritual body. When the Sadducee is referred to as not believing in God, Angel, or Spirit, Angel and Spirit are distinguished; spirits are disembodied for a season, but angels are clothed upon and glorified in spiritual bodies. It is mystery; and so is it that the Jeweler takes a watch apart, repairs it, inserts a new main spring, restores all the parts, easily, to their proper places, winds it, and on it goes; you or I could neither do nor comprehend the repairs.

II.

Having considered objections and prepared the way, we come directly to Revelation. It teaches that the body that died shall be resurrected and fashioned like Christ's body in His ascension, and rejoined to its own spirit forever.

1. St. Paul's illustration of the wheat assists us in comprehending its certainty, but not its mystery. The grain is sown which starts up the rising germ, and all the nutritive portion of the old grain, except the envelope or bran enters into the budding plant. But the new plant though initiated in the sown seed, assumes, by and by, blades, stalk, flowers and fruited ears. These are not in the ground

as was the old seed, but have risen up, and stand in the light, and wave in the breeze. Many seeds discover, by the microscope, a small perfect form of the future plant. The entire plant is hundreds of times larger than the seed and by no means resembles it. Paul's theory is that the seed must die, then from it and of it, God gives a body to the new plant.

Paul's next illustration asserts that "all flesh is not the same flesh;" that of men, beasts, fishes and birds being quite different. Had one never seen nor heard of a bird, he would fearlessly say there could not be bird, or life with wings to inhabit the air. Had one never known of fish, he would aver there could be no fish, or animal monster inhabiting water. But God's variety and power in the production of animal life have utterly confounded unbelief. The mighty revelations by the microscope, of the infinite multitude of life in the water drops and microcosms of all nature, do clearly tell us God can do anything. And so variable is all flesh, that if a particle of bone, invisible to the naked eye, be tested by the microscope, the animal to which it belonged can be accurately delineated.

3. Paul then intimates that while terrestrial

bodies, or the bodies of living men are dull, weighty, sickly, earthly, inglorious, on the other hand celestial bodies or the bodies of Enoch, Elijah, Angels perhaps, CHRIST, and all other heavenly life which has spiritual body enveloping spirit, are light, buoyant, healthful, heavenly and glorious. The bodily effulgence there, shall be as the spiritual holiness here. Its corruption is gone, because dissolution and death are ended; its weakness passes away because age, wasting and decay are no more; its natural, fleshly combination is changed because its functions and reproductions cease to be earthly; but its perfect, spiritual, indestructible form is now entered upon. The present form of flesh and blood, the weakness, the corruption, cannot inherit immortality. Even the living who live to the judgment must be changed, fashioned like those resurrected. They do not die, they do not leave the body, but simply suffer a change.

4. Nature furnishes analogies: yonder caterpillar is a worm, unsightly and perishable. By and by it weaves a shroud and enters into the long sleep of the chrysalis. Then its sleep is ended. It comes forth full formed, the butterfly, winged and beautiful, a new creature, living upon the hon-

ey of the flower. It is the former caterpillar resurrected and made glorious, flying far away from its grave and the worm-hood of its first existence. God can do all things, and his positive revelation settles all controversy. As day succeeds night, as Spring succeeds Winter, as butterflies succeed caterpillars, so the probability and the feasibility of the immortal succeeding the mortal is made into a certainty.

5. To the Word again. Job says, "If a man die shall he live again?" or emphatically "he *shall* live again." Further says he, "I will wait till my change come." "There is hope of a tree if it be cut down that it will sprout again, and that the tender branch therof will not cease." So when the heavens should be no more and God's wrath be overpast, Job was confident of being remembered, God's Spirit meantime inditing the doctrine.

6. Ezekiel, in his valley of dry bones, prophesied of Israel's restoration; but the figure of illustration was clearly taken from the admitted circumstances of a resurrection fully believed among the Jews. The breath came upon the dry bones and a great multitude stood up and shook off the

dust and went home from their land of banishment. There is no pertinence in this vision, unless it be the inspired confirmation of the doctrine of the resurrection of the human body.

7. Says Daniel, "Many of them that sleep in the dust of the earth shall awake, some to everlasting life." In all his clear imagery, Daniel has not enunciated a clearer intention than this of final resurrection.

David says, "God shall redeem my soul from the power of the grave;" and affirms elsewhere "I shall be satisfied when I awake with thy likeness."

Job answers back from the old time, "I know that my redeemer liveth * * In my flesh I shall see God."

The great and learned Paul says before Felix, "The Jews themselves allow that there will be a resurrection of the dead."

After Paul, let us hear the greater Christ. Lazarus had died, and the resurrection must be demonstrated. The Master talks with Martha; the comfortable doctrine is enunciated, "He that believeth in me, though he were dead, yet shall he live." Then the demonstration follows, and Lazarus is made to come forth from the sleep of death.

But go consult exulting apostles and shouting prophets; go ask the widow of Zarephath; go commune with the Shunamite on Mt. Carmel; see the daughter of Jairus, the ruler; inquire of the widow of Nain. All these have seen their dead raised, and personal identity was perfect and natural. These and hundreds of other cases clearly demonstrate GOD'S power and plan, the soul's immortality and the body's resurrection. If the power of GOD can recall the soul to a man dead four days, it can also raise him when dead four thousand years.

> "I know the time shall come
> When through the charnel dumb,
> A voice shall ring upon the slumbering ear:
> These bones shall startle then
> And feel strange life again
> And these decaying fibres leap to hear."

III.

Having dwelt upon the general scriptural doctrine of the resurrection, we now proceed to fortify its certainty by the blessed and comforting example of CHRIST'S resurrection. In this portion we have freely consulted Watson, Wesley, Adam Clarke, Mattison, and Bishops Clark and Kingsley. Our argument will connect the Christian sleeping with CHRIST in death, to the CHRIST who by His power also shook asunder death's prison and ascended to the city of mansions. If we find CHRIST arose, then we know He will execute His ample provisions, in the quickening of all His saints. So important is this connection that our resurrection is proven by CHRIST'S resurrection; without His, ours would fail; with His, ours is pledged and certain.

1. Was there an incarnate CHRIST?

The Bible is a biography and prophecy of CHRIST and His works. Profane history makes us as absolutely certain of His incarnation and existence as of Napoleon's. Josephus, Justin Martyr, and Tertullian, as well as His enemies, Julian, Celsus and Porphyry, all confirm His nature, and life, and death.

2. Should this divine person ever die? Yes, this was His special mission, so the prophets clearly certify; and further CHRIST should be the identical rising CHRIST. All the types of Jewish law

symbolize Him; all the sacrifices affirmed His death from the "Lamb without spot" and the innocent "Turtle-dove" to Isaac on Mt. Moriah. His birth at Bethlehem was declared, His descent from the seed of Judah was discriminated and with transgressors He was numbered in His death, centuries in advance. CHRIST, in the New Testament, proclaimed often His own death. "Destroy this Temple and in three days I will raise it up." John says "He spake this of the temple of his body." It was a fact well known, that He said "After three days I will rise.

3. *The fulfillment.* He was put to death and buried in Josephs' new tomb. So his enemies all admit; so the Roman soldiers officially announce to Pilate; so the centurion doubly authenticated; Jews were witnesses of the fact; seals were added to the rock; guards were stationed; death was assisted in his tomb imprisonment by armed soldiers. Pilate said "make it sure as ye can."

4. Did He rise? Ask the weeping Marys who appeared on Sabbath morning to embalm the CRUCIFIED, when no body was there. Ask the Angels who were there as witnesses of the resurrection. Ask the Soldier guard who could not at the peril

of life account for the absent JESUS. The broken seals, the open sepulcher, and the terrified soldiers, were all certain witnesses of super-natural escape. Nor could any Roman fabrication allay public opinion of the miracle. Did disciples steal Him? Physical and moral impossibility! impossibility without motive in the attempt! Could sixty soldiers on guard, all be asleep, at the peril of life? If so how did they know of the theft? Would eleven timid, unarmed fishermen presume upon their slumbers in so rash a deed? If they did, why not arrest and punish the thieving disciples, these body lifters, when immediately they were publicly preaching the resurrection, to the conversion of thousands. Jewry and Græcia were full of independent thought, philosophical investigation and skepticism; they absolutely craved novel things, that they might logically prove their falsity. But mark, except the Sadducees who will not believe in resurrection, no creed, philosophy, nor sect, for centuries, dared to deny the fact of CHRIST'S resurrection.

5. He appeared frequently in person to His followers.

(1.) By the Sabbath morning twilight of the first

Easter Sunday, Mary Magdalene had, at the tomb, the first recognition of the Risen Lord, who said tenderly to her: "Mary." (Let women have license to preach JESUS in the pulpit and vote religion at the ballot box; for the testimony was first committed to her of the resurrection, and being less skeptical, she is more devout than man.)

(2.) The other Mary and Salome meet the LORD next, and are entrusted with His first official message, "Go tell my brethren that they go into Galilee and there shall they see me."

(3.) Soon after, Joanna and other women went by another direction to the tomb, for embalming purposes, when two angels said to them, "He is not here, He is risen." These glad women quickly told Peter who ran to see for himself, and probably this was the time when the LORD "was seen of Cephas."

(4.) In the forenoon, up toward Emmaus, two disciples were journeying home from the passover, thinking all was lost. By the way, the RISEN LORD fell in company, expounded the prophecies of His own resurrection, and finally made Himself known unto them.

(5) That Sabbath evening prayer meeting was

being held. The stirring events of the day were discussed in the social meeting which followed, and amid the wavering faith of some and the despair of others, suddenly the SAVIOUR'S voice and person in their midst said: "Peace be unto you."

(6.) Eight days later, the next Sabbath evening, Thomas was at the prayer meeting; he was skeptical; he needed special treatment, and, sure enough, the LORD appeared as before with benedictions of "Peace," and said to doubting Thomas, "Behold my hands; and reach hither thy hand and thrust it into my side."

(7.) Later, the disciples resorted to their Galilee homes and resumed their nets. A night's labor caught nothing, but at dawn, a stranger on the shore said: "Cast the net on the right side," and, behold, a miracle of fishes came into the net; they knew it was JESUS; and they were soon eating with Him on the shore.

(8.) Soon after, at a grove meeting, appointed before the crucifixion, on a mountain, above five hundred were assembled in worship. And, behold, JESUS appeared in their midst and they worshiped Him there.

(9.) He was also seen of James as mentioned in Paul's collection of his manifestations.

(10.) Finally, forty days after the tragedy of His death, He met the disciples by appointment in Jerusalem. Then, to that blessed Mount of Olives, near the city, He led them. Then, after their commission to the ministry was given, and the HOLY GHOST was promised, He lifted up His hands and blessed them, and while blessing them He rose up, in that posture, into heaven out of their sight.

This is our testimony. Could there be doubt? His disciples were many and competent witnesses; and they died martyrs in testimony of belief in these events. They suddenly became bold witnesses of the resurrection, over all the traveled world. They wrought miracles in the name of CHRIST; and to this day the power and presence of a Risen SAVIOUR are converting the world.

Group the facts. CHRIST, on the cross, submitted to death; CHRIST, from the tomb, took up His own life powerfully, boldly, triumphantly. This event becomes cause; and the resurrection of his family becomes effect. "Now *is* CHRIST risen from the dead and become the first fruits of them that slept." He is the first ripe sheaf of the coming harvest. He is the pledge and proof that the harvest of the resurrection will surely come.

Bishop Kingsley derives three important reflections from the event of Christ's resurrection. They guard us against the modern scientist's doctrine that literal resurrection is a delusion. The substance briefly, is as follows:

1. The same literal body of JESUS that lived and was crucified, also arose and ascended. JESUS' literal body was sought in the tomb, but found not. His literal body was seen afterwards having nail-prints and spear-wounds. Disciples held His literal feet afterward and worshiped. His literal body ate broiled fish with them. Did He wish to deceive them when He addressed those who thought literal resurrection impossible? Was He only a spirit when He said "Handle me, and see, for a spirit hath not flesh and bones as ye see me have"?

2. Either CHRIST had a literal body after resurrection, or He deceived His followers; but it is impossible that He deceived His followers, therefore CHRIST had a literal body, as he intended them to believe.

3. CHRIST'S resurrected body was the same that ascended. It suffered no change to the disciples

until the final scene of the ascension. From the sad and loving countenance marred by the crown of thorns down to the feet identified by nail-prints, it was the same crucified body which went up into heaven out of their sight.

CONCLUSION.

The Bible doctrine and the Christian faith, then, involve the following future scenes which will surely come to pass :

Scene 1st. GOD'S family, who now sleep in death shall end their slumbers, at a time unknown to men or angels. Hence those who assert that the end of the world is at any fixed date, have no Bible authority and are idle deceivers. While the special date was wisely withheld from man as a motive for him to be always ready, yet the general intimations are that the gospel must be preached to all nations before the end come. Even in CHRIST'S time, He called the age "last days" intimating thus that the world was on the second half of its destiny.

Scene 2nd. The official announcement of this event to angels and the universe will be the trumpet blast of Gabriel.

Scene 3d. CHRIST, then, accompanied by hosts of angels and the disembodied souls which He has redeemed, shall assemble in mid air.

Scene 4th. The trumpet of GOD shall signal the next eventful crisis, namely; the original bodies that have died in all time, shall come forth from their graves, and shall then and there be re-fashioned, glorified and re-united with the waiting souls which CHRIST brought with him. This scene will be an era of gladness to the souls of the martyrs and the good of all ages. Ashes will take forms of glory from the stake, bruised bodies from the rack, and submerged forms from the ocean.

Scene 5th. After this preference of time to the dead, then those who are alive at that day, of GOD's family, in their natural bodies, shall, in the twinkling of an eye, be changed into immortal bodies which the spirits can never leave, so that they shall be precisely like the ones resurrected; and the whole saved host will then have bodies like to that of CHRIST.

Scene 6th. With a burning world beneath them and an assembled universe around, the legal investigation of a judgment will occur. The righteous will be assembled in one vast throng and will now begin to "shine as the brightness of the firmament." The legal investigation upon the faith and works of men will be just and faithful, neither tardy nor hasty.

Scene 7th. The wicked who are not of GOD's family, will again be cumbered with the law of gravitation, so that they are helpless, except to sink down to some appointed place where GOD has never spoken light, and there gravity will hold soul and body forever.

Scene 8th. The righteous, or GOD's family, formerly of earth, whom we have traced from the work and faith of probation, through the dusty sleep of death to the quickening of immortality, shall now be crowned and fitted with a heavenly outfit of palms of victory and harps of glory; and, free from gravity, free to roam GOD's universe, they shall be conducted up through the gates to Heaven's capital to be in felicity forever.

This event closes the scenes of the resurrection. The curtain drops; the mortal and immortal, heaven and earth, time and eternity are conjoined. Labor is ended; death itself is dead; joy is begun; day is eternal; and happy elysium around the throne of GOD and over the City of Mansions, among angels, will certify to the redeemed, the fullness of eternal life.

CHRIST having literally and bodily risen, and having left his promises for his people, let the fever-wasted, consumption-tossed, dying saint take hope, for he shall rise again. Let the snow of winter envelope the body of the departed, let the dust sleep sweetly in its original dust, it shall rise again. Let the Angel of the final day ring all earth's atmosphere with his solemn blast, it is the harbinger of eternal life. Let earth, with its cities, and fruitful land, and rolling ocean be enveloped in dissolving fires, the flames cannot touch the bodies of saints when a fourth like the SON OF GOD is in their midst. Let the OMEGA of "time no longer" complete the solemn diapason; it will not now be a requiem of saints, but their final jubilee out of the dust of the earth. Let the CRUCIFIED set His throne of Judgment in the air, it is only to issue a royal proclamation to His martyred, time-tossed children who die no more, "Come thou blessed of my FATHER, inherit the kingdom." Let angels who inhabit heaven, be attracted by the cry of a doomed world to witness the final scene, they will take home a new and saved brotherhood of saints into their eternal joy.

It will be enough. The saints will say they are satisfied when the eternal snmmer of God, in His own homestead, shall succeed time's winter and welcome with heaven's bliss.

Do you believe it, dear, discouraged, dying saint? Do you doubt the word? Do you waver at the power of God? Take courage; cheer up; be glad even now, for Christ has already gone to prepare the mansions. He will come again; get ready to go; have your heart full of hope, of grace, of righteousness. Cling to the cross. You are immortal. You shall rise again.

"THESE ARE THEY." Rev. vii: 14.

CHAPTER V.

God's Family in its Heavenly Home.

OR

Saints and Angels Consolidated.

"NEITHER can they die any more; for they are equal unto the angels; and are the children of God, being the children of the resurrection." Luke xx. 36.

By the old Latin Testament of Theodora Beza of 1556, and also the old Greek Testament of Greenfield of 1624, we make the following liberal translation of the above: "For they are not able to die any more; for they are equal to the angels; and they are the sons of God, since they are the sons of the resurrection."

The new shade of thought which these add to the common English version is this: being the sons of the resurrection and unable to die any more, they are fully and properly now the sons of God. Since God is the God of the living, therefore they are equal to the angels.

Now we gather very much more of the nature of angels than of these redeemed and resurrected sons of God who are their equals. If then our word "*equal*" signifies general identity of qualities and we can more easily and better describe *angels*, we will have described *saints* in their post-resurrection estate. The more do we prefer this analogous method, inasmuch as angels are a large and legitimate part of the heavenly family, and must be described to complete our task.

Let us first however allude to the family Home. Heaven is the Old Homestead of God and His family. His outside children are wanderers. Heaven is, according to the Scriptures, a fixed, pure, ample, holy, and glorious world. It is Home, for Father is there; it is Home, Jesus is there; it is Home, Angels are there; it is Home, saints abide there forever. Revelation, written in human language, does not and cannot describe it, save by faint comparison with earthly places. Human language and human comprehension are both limited. It were idle and useless, even in an angel, to reveal the utterly incomprehensible, to a weak mortal. Heaven's description has rather been a negative one. The obnoxious of earth is forever banished from heaven; sin, disease, change, unhappiness, all that distresses, and death are banished from heaven forever. Man can comprehend a negative description. Going from this to the positive side, our conceptions are put upon the path by comparison with earth's most agreeable characteristics. Immortality, Spirituality, holy associations, the Sabbath day and its worship made eternal, satisfying plenty, peace, rest, enjoyment, are only Bible glimpses of Heaven. After thus making the highest comparisons which earth could yield, or man comprehend, the Bible assures us that heaven is beyond conception, that the highest imagination of gorgeous felicity is far less than Heaven's reality and glory. It is full of mansions, centrally washed by a river of life, fruited by trees with healing leaves, paved with gold, walled with precious stones, feasted on manna, harmonized by music, spiritualized by flaming fire, lighted by a shining throne, centralized by GOD's capital, rapt with the presence of JESUS, populated with saints and angels. But poor language faints, and falters, and fails, and yonder hill country of light is past description. This is the Homestead of GOD.

We return to the family. It consists of GOD, Angels and Saints. The two latter are alike. They may differ in origin, in place and time of nativity, in heavenly age, in wisdom, in previous condition and in present relation to the TRINITY. But in privileges, in purity, in form, in immortality, in employment, in enjoyment, in characteristics of soul, in theological views, in perceptions of truth, in beautiful righteousness, in blessed perfections, they are similar. Our Latin "pares," Greek "isos" and English "equal" justify these conclusions. The difference among saints and angels in their post-resurrective state, need be no more than the diversity in a large earthly family. There will be individual diversities, but a residence, side by sidè, far into eternity, will tend to unify diversities. Let us inquire

I. *What are Angels?*

The Hebrew word *Mălák* from the Hebrew root *Lak* and the Arabic *Kylack* and the Ethiopic '*Olack* signifies "one that ministers," one that waits upon," "one sent," "a messenger." The Greek is ἄγγελος, from the verb ἀγγέλλω, the Latin *Angelus*, the German, Dutch, Danish and Swedish *engel*, Portuguese *anjo*, Spanish *angel*, Italian *angelo*, French *ange*, Old Irish *aingeal*, English *angel.* The literal signification is, *a messenger*, *one who* carries news. Homer applied it in the language of poetry to *birds*, which in his fable were *prognostications.* In the language of love, angel often signifies *a very amiable person.* In the Scriptures it has the following senses. 1. *An Embassador of God.* 2. In the usual and more general sense *a Spirit or Spiritual intelligence employed of the Almighty in His stead to communicate His will to man.* 3. It is *a minister of God to minister to man.* 4. It is *a being sent to execute God's judgments.* Beneath these usual senses in an evil sense it may be, 5. *An evil Spirit loose on a bad errand against man, from the bottomless pit.* Above the usual sense, it rises up to 6. *Christ the Great Angel of the Covenant, the Mediator, and Head of the Church.* Such titles in the Old Testament as "The Angel of the Covenant," "Angel of the LORD," "Angel of JEHOVAH," the "*Mălak Jĕhovah*" are undoubtedly manifestations of DEITY himself, the "Son" or "Second Person" of the Trinity, foreshadowing his final incarnation to Abraham, Moses and the Prophets.

Omitting all these extraordinary uses of the term we confine ourselves now to that common and frequent use which interprets and limits it to celestial intelligences having homes in heaven, and revealed to us incidentally, when sent on missions to earth.

II. *Voice of the Church on the nature of Angels, for eighteeen centuries.*

Many of the fathers after the days of the apostles, nay most of them, held that angels were created beings and ministering spirits. Some ascribed bodies to them, of finer substance than human bodies. For three centuries after CHRIST, no one proposed worship to them, as the Romanists now do.

Justin Martyr thought them personal beings having a personal existence. He attached importance to the theory that they had bodies analogous to that of man. Manna was their food. Clement said "They have neither ears nor tongue nor lips nor organs of respiration." Tatien said: "These etherial bodies of angels can be perceived by those in whom the Spirit of GOD dwells." Tertulian says: "Si corporis alicujus, sui tamen generis."—"if of any body, then of their own peculiar kind."

From the middle of the third century to the

middle of the seventh, when the heresy of Arius suggested that CHRIST was a creature, like the angels, giving rise to the modern doctrine of Unitarianism, a sharp line was drawn, showing that angels were created *creatures* rather than *aeons* eminating from GOD's essence as some few suggested. They were regarded as quite superior to man, worthy of reverence, but not of adoration, unless St. Ambrose be excepted. He recommended their invocation. Gregory thought them created prior to the rest of the world. Augustine thought them created on the first day of our creation. Basil calls them "*Aerion pneuma, pur aulon*," an aerial spirit, a flaming fire;" he therefore thinks they have a certain bodily form. Gregory supposes them divine servants, with a power partly original and partly derived, all acting in and by the one will of the Creator. Augustine calls them "domestics of GOD, citizens of heaven, chiefs of Paradise, masters of knowledge, doctors of wisdom, illuminators of souls, protectors and guardians of the good." (We translate his Latin.) Fulgentius says "they are body and spirit, knowing GOD by the latter and appearing to men by the former." Gregory of Nazianzen says they are limited spirits without bodies, while GOD is unlimited." It was generally admitted that angels were free to stand or fall until the fall of the evil angels, when the steadfast ones, many contended, had a certain knowledge and warning which fixed them invulnerable.

From the eighth to the sixteenth century, the Church accorded a more spiritual nature to angels. They agreed that angels were not of a race or species, but each spoken into existence alone without a brotherhood, and hence, that any action, as sin, if it were possible, could not affect any other angel.

Anselm says "There is a human race, but not an angelic race."

The sixteenth century distinguished angels from the souls of men. They need no body as men do; they do not obtain knowledge by inference, but by intuition; they do not think by means of images, but by intuition; they are probably fixed in their moral estate; they have a language not of sense, but intellectual.

From 1556 to 1700, both Protestants and Romanists scripturally believed in angels. Yet Romanists prayed to angels, while Protestants did not. Luther was ultra in ascribing very great attributes to angels and especially to devils. You remember in his conflicts with Satan he thought him omnipresent.

The Church from 1700 to the present, have generally with much caution, rested an opinion of angels upon scriptural grounds. Swedenbourg has fallen into the grossest materialism on the subject. He says "Angels breathe as well as men; their hearts also beat." He affirms all angels derive their origin from the human race. Lange as unscripturally concludes that angels are the spirits of the primeval world. Such has been the faith of the Church about angels.

III. *The Scriptural doctrine.*

Dr. Smith says "They are created, therefore finite beings. If finite, they are progressive. If progressive, they are voluntary. If voluntary, they have capacity for temptation, but are infinitely removed from any liability to temptation.

According to St. Jude, some of them were tempted and fell. Theologically their state is fixed with absoluteness, and yet they have voluntary possibility.

The nature in us which thinks, reasons, hopes, fears, rejoices, weeps, worships and loves, in a word, the soul part, if it could be divested of this earthly body, or at least could be clothed with heaven's habitude, the spiritual body, would then become what the angel appears to be. The angel is one such as we will be, in most particulars, perhaps in all, with, however, his probation over, immortality achieved, and the heavenly home and the freedom of the universe inherited, and the hovel of some margin, some outskirt of the circle of light exchanged for its central city. It is plausible from human analogy, though not asserted in the Scriptures, that angels may have been originally created like ourselves on some planet of some solar system, or rather upon several, and when their probation ended, that they were exalted, as the righteous will be, to the great family in Heaven. We do not assert this, but suggest its possibility.

If they once had different habitations, as Cherubim from one primal home, Seraphim from another, Principalities from another, Powers from another, Gabriel from another, and Michael from another, they have certainly become gloriously unified, in Scripture times. They present the same qualities to mortals, except ordinary individual diversities. We suggest it theologically probable, that no creature would be at once introduced to Heaven without an outer probation. And if, in that angelic probation of first existence, they suffered a fall, as we did, it would be like the SON of GOD to "fly to the relief" of other worlds than ours. Of this we know not; our Revelation is only for this world and the relation of CHRIST to us. Yet says CHRIST "Other sheep I have which are not of this fold." Were they gentiles, or were they other fallen and redeemed worlds?

But we return to the Scriptural allusions.

(*a*) A clear angel, like other angels, performing the mission of an angel, appeared to the Revelator on Patmos. That angel would not accept worship from John, but to avoid such idolatry, or rather angelatry, he revealed his own former existence by saying: "I am thy fellow servant, and of thy brethren the prophets." What a similarity, a brotherhood between John and the angel. The difference was that the angel, once of earth, now a common inhabitant of Heaven, had come to bear testimony of JESUS, while John was yet an inhabitant of earth, detained a little while from Heaven to bear the same testimony of JESUS.

(*b*) A group of Sadducees tempt the SAVIOUR of

the world. They narrate the case of a woman who had seven brethren as husbands. He who spake as never man spake, said of the men and women who reach Heaven: "They are equal unto the angels." They are like the angels. The reverse of this announcement must be true, viz. angels are like the men and women who enter immortality.

(*c*) Understandest thou the spirit which lives, and burns and longs for immortality within thee? Nay; the very spirit of man is inexplicable in its essence. The essence of angelic nature must be still more so, since removed by one step, from a subjective to an objective reality. The full solution of the angel would be to establish the identity of man when he enters immortality.

This objection is made to our brotherhood with angels: If men in Heaven and angels already there are precisely similar in essence and all else striking, save previous history, what satisfactory explanation can be Scripturally suggested of the nature or essence of the resurrected body of men which will be similar to that of angels? We reply: The Scriptures do not determine the nature of the Scriptural body with which angels are clothed and the human may be much more nearly similar to the angelic body than at first supposed.

Illustrations may show how men may approach very near angelic life, although the question of pure spirit and spiritual body may divide.

(*a*) Nothing is impossible with God.

(*b*) Bodies of both men and animals upon exchange of climate on earth become acclimated.

(*c*) Bodies of different habits diminish or increase by fifty or a hundred pounds in a few weeks.

(*d*) The traveler from the cold north, across the lines of latitude, to the equator, is first covered with heavy weights of clothing to combat the frigidness of cold. But soon the outer layer of covering may be cast off; and as he moves southward another and another of the thick garments is dispensed with, until by and by, under the shadowless sun, he stands in the thin white garments usual in the tropics. So with the man immortal, when from earth he rises to the world of light.

(*e*) The three Hebrews were not subject to the usual laws of combustion from the energy of fire, when a fourth like the Son of God was so near them. Miracles to us may be natural law to God.

(*f*) So in the resurrection, Deity will resuscitate the spirit covering which rested in gross matter since death. That much, is spiritual body. The total avoirdupois is not the consideration; but the fact of the victory of life over death, the triumph over the grave, the restoration into immortality, of just what otherwise was to become the spiritual body by translation, if death had never entered; these are really the test questions of man's resurrection.

(*g*) When David strolls, by night, under the canopy of GOD's blue, to contrast GOD's Heavens with his own insignificance, he is rapt in the announcement " When I consider the heavens " and continues " what is man ?" " Thou hast made him a little lower than the angels." The original is: " Thou hast made him for a little time less than the Elohim," or GOD spirit, the Great Angel. And then the divine coronation comes in prospect; " Thou hast crowned him with glory and honor." " Lower than the angels," how lower ? Not in essence, not in power of soul, not in form of body, but in fact of probation, in time of detention from the angel home; not lower than angels once were but lower than they now are " for a little time." All these illustrations assist in the comprehension of angelic natures, and reconcile men and angels into a brotherhood.

How can a spiritual body, how can the risen JESUS, pass through bars and doors and stand in the midst, beyond material barriers? Such is another objection. These gross eyes of ours lead to very gross conclusions. The chemistry of matter reveals it very porous, that atoms do not touch each other, that gaseous bodies, as hydrogen, may escape without inconvenience from ordinary vessels, that a small bulk of gas might suddenly expand into a space infinitely greater than its common rarity and fill that space, that rays of light may move one hundred and eighty-two thousand miles per second, pierce the retina without harm, and make pictures upon the very brain, that light may plunge through deep water, solid glass, or any transparency, and move on its journey unretarded. May not the spiritual body, free as an angel, delivered from the laws of gravity, like a ray of light, fresh from Heaven, dart readily through solids and deep earth? Yes, if GOD prepare that body for that end.

IV. *The variety of Angels.*

The order of Heaven has declared no titles

of nobility among its angels, but the work in Heaven is systematized so that there is division of labor.

(*a*) Michael the Archangel is foremost. There can be but one archangel, one greatest. He has no rival. The name signifies "He who is like God." He is therefore

> "Brightest and best of the sons of the morning."

He is the leader of the host of light, in God's name, against the devil. His strength is opposed to Satan's strength. Especially when the people Israel fought against godless heathen, if Satan is represented as aiding their enemies, then Michael is among their friends. In Daniel (x : 13) an angel spoke kindly to the prophet saying "But the prince of the kingdom of Persia withstood me one and twenty days; but lo! *Michael*, one of the chief princes, came to help me;" again, "There is none that holdeth with me in these things but *Michael* your prince;" and again, "At that time shall *Michael* stand up." Thus Michael is the warrior of God against Satan and in favor of the Jews. In Jude (9th verse) we find Michael disputing with the devil about the body of Moses, perhaps concealing

Moses' body so the Jews would not worship his tomb. In Revelations (xii. 7-9) is this record, "And there was war in heaven, Michael and his angels fought against the dragon; and the dragon fought and his angels, and prevailed not; neither was there place found any more in heaven. And the great dragon was cast out, that old serpent called the devil, and Satan which deceiveth the whole world; he was cast out into the earth, and his angels were cast out with him." These five passages include all that is said of the Archangel; but from his name and his mission these facts appear: 1. He was in GOD's place to the Jews. 2. He was especially commissioned to reconnoiter the works of the devil.

(*b*) Next is Gabriel. The name is "*Might of God.*" He is thus introduced, (Dan. viii. 16), "And I heard a man's voice between the banks of Ulai, which called and said, Gabriel make this man to understand the vision." He soon appears to Daniel and unfolds the mystery of the seventy weeks. Gabriel also tells Zacharias and Mary, that the fullness of time was come, that John the Forerunner and JESUS the MESSIAH are about to appear. Gabriel is therefore evidently the angel of comfort and sympathy to man. His final duty will be to call the nations to judgment.

(*c*) Then are Cherubim. The Hebrew signifies "*like the powerful one.*" They are emblems to us of that part of GOD's family of angels, which represent in coldness, His justice. They are not messengers of sympathy, but of divine wrath and judgment. They guarded the gates of Eden forfeited, with flaming swords, as sentinels of GOD. They appear to Ezekiel (i. 10), in the very remarkable vision of the wheels of the ALMIGHTY, inspiring awe by their vast burning presence and wonderful form. They stood close to the visible Shechinah, over the ark of the Mercy Seat, to see that the typical law was vindicated to the letter.

(*d*) Next are Seraphim. The word signifies "*exalted,*" in the Arabic, and in the Hebrew, "*Burning.*" The Seraphim come a little nearer the poor heart of humanity than the Cherubim. They bring live coals from the burning, heavenly altar, and touch the unclean lips of Isaiah, making him clean and willing to work. Their emblem is holiness. They cry, "Holy, holy, holy is the LORD OF HOSTS."

(*e*) Finally are the general multitude of angels, the common messengers of heaven.

They will assist us to know more of heaven than all the others, for they are the rank and file of heaven. A man from the dusty fields of his agriculture, betrays, by that dust, his employment. A honey-bee, by the sweet odors it bears, and the pollen and honey that line and cover its limbs, says clearly that it has been in the blossoming fields and gardens. So an angel, by the pure, sweet, solemn mission, and by the bright glory that is brushed from its wings, says plainly that it has brushed these emblems from the Hesperus gardens that line and beautify the Paradise along life's river; the glory dust is on its wings.

V. *Their manifestations.*

Angels are messengers of love, protection, warning, and prophecy.

(*a*) The first angels on record ever speaking to mortal, brought comfort to Hagar at the fountain in the wilderness, as she fled the bitterness of home.

(*b*) Then they appear in the tent door to Abraham as strangers, and he entertains angels unawares, and thereby learns of the child of promise, and also of the fall of Sodom.

(*c*) Then they visit Lot and rescue him, and

burn the wicked city of the plain, bringing both mercy and judgment.

(*d*) They visit Hagar again, and tell in comfort of the coming greatness of Ishmael.

(*e*) Then they ascend and descend Jacob's ladder in multitudes to the joy of the Patriarch.

(*f*) They appear to Jacob on the journey and he said, "This is GOD's host," and he called the place "Mahanaim," "the two hosts or camps," the host of GOD and the host of Esau.

(*g*) An angel wrestled with the patriarch until morning when his name was changed to *Israel*, or *Prince of God.*

(*h*) Then they are silent while GOD Himself works for Israel in the days of Moses; yet the "Angel of the LORD" goes before and fights for Israel.

(*i*) In Canaan, an angel meets and opposes Balaam in the way.

(*j*) After a wide interval they come again; one at Bochim reproves Israel; another strengthens Gideon against Midian; another appears to Manoah and acts wondrously, rising to heaven on the flame of the sacrifice.

(*k*) A mighty throng of angels light down

about the hills of Dothan and appear to the deliverance of Elisha and his servant.

(*l*) A single angel, full of power, interposes for Hezekiah, and slays in one night the entire thousands of Sennacherib.

(*m*) Space would fail to tell how GOD's angels "encamp around them that fear Him;" how "The chariots of GOD are twenty thousand, even thousands of angels;" how the angels that excel in strength do bless GOD; how "He maketh his angels spirits, his ministers a flaming fire;" how "The angel of his presence saved Zion;" how "He sent his angel to 'deliver from the fiery furnace and also to shut the lions' mouths."

(*n*) Then comes the "Angel of the Covenant," the "Messiah," the Second Person of the Trinity at the Incarnation, and the entire host leave the Beatitudes and sing in mid-air, "Glory to GOD in the Highest, on earth peace, good will toward men." Legions of them attended the incarnate SAVIOUR, and in the temptation "When the devil left him, angels came and ministered to him."

(*o*) Angels are to be the Reapers in the Harvest of the world; angels are the guardians of the little ones, who always behold the face of the FATHER;

God's church "are not come to Mount Sinai, but unto Mount Sion and to an innumerable company of angels;" in a word, they are "all ministering spirits sent forth to minister to them who shall be heirs of salvation."

(*p*) In the wonderful series of visions on Patmos, where the Book of Revelation was sealed, and the things that should come to pass were manifest, angels were thick in the scheme. So in the closing scenes of earth they will gather to witness the tragedy.

The absence of angels, in the intervals when God spake face to face with man, and when also the gospel was a sufficient guide, is no proof of their real absence. They are more concealed now, there is no open vision, God's word is sufficiently precious in these days.

> "Angels now are hov'ring round us,
> Unperceived amid the throng;
> Wond'ring at the love that crowned us,
> Glad to join the holy song."

On earth angels minister in the natural and supernatural to man. Since they are said to look into the mysteries of redemption, they hasten, they fly to do the will of the Highest to us-ward in the advancement of that plan. In the old Testament their mission was to Israel and his people, and the people who led him into captivity; in the New Testament their mission is to single individuals. When they stand at the Sepulcher and tell Mary that CHRIST is risen, it is the most thrilling news that angel ever communicated. And it is plausible that the Resurrection was first known by angels. They were there, no doubt, within the ring of the Roman guard and witnessed the very event of JESUS stepping forth from the grave.

After CHRIST'S resurrection they are, incidentally, mentioned very frequently, as the invariable attendants of GOD'S children and perhaps of all the human family Wesley thinks it probable that many of the events of our lives are affected by the angels that guard us. In their mission of ministering spirits, Revelation has disclosed most about them. They are often commissioned and instructed delegates from heaven and home, yet they are not outlaws, but most loyal subjects of GOD.

Ages ago Hessiod said "Millions of spirits walk the earth unseen." The knowledge, purity, holiness and sympathy of angels is incomprehensible to fallen, weak man. How much they counteract and oppose demons that would harm us, we cannot tell. How much they may command the well being of our bodies in times of danger or disease, is only to be inferred. With their great comprehension, they can "touch the secret main-springs of being, with a finger of power, by God's permission," to cause life and health to our organism.

They are a very large part of the Family of God. They act in harmony with God. Their work is the work of God, though done by angels. Their final earthly mission to man, so far as made known, is to carry the spirits of the good to Paradise.

VI. *The Sequel.*

Recall now our proposition at the outset.

1. We stated that the Heavenly Family would be God and the consolidated saints and angels with uniform similarities save individual diversities.

2. Since the Scriptures have presented very many exhibitions of angels and of the redeemed only in prospect after the resurrection, our task would be better accomplished by describing the angel rather than the saint. This done, we now affirm the redeemed are to be like the angels in all

except previous history and other minor particulars.

The judgment day brings to the righteous full fellowship and joy with angels. Whatever, therefore, will, to all eternity, attach to angels, of qualities, duties and joys, will equally attach forever to immortal saints. As some vast colony of the West has its emigrants at different times, from New England, New York, Pennsylvania, the South, and from across the seas, Germany, France and Italy, and all these in time become one, in language, heart, Americanized institutions, interests and destiny, so in heaven, earth's good will be colonized and beautified into one glorious, immortal community, in the eternal city, centering around one palace of light and God Blessed forevermore. Here then is the Eden above, the Canaan over the river, the Heavenly Jerusalem, the Church Triumphant, the Eternal Sabbath, the Living Fountain. It is not far off, as God and angels count distance, nor will the consummation of our joy be long delayed. He who has no land here, except six feet by two in the valley of rest, there, over there, has home, mansion and FATHER.

The Church Militant is full of probationers. In

the Church Triumphant they are taken into full connection. All its mighty, free, holy, happy, intelligence, with heaven as home, and a universe as a field of investigation, go right on in the high and deep themes of Theology, of life immortal, of nature of self. They may visit the ruins of earth and the rolling scroll of the passing heavens to the very borders of light in distant space. Wherever presence may go, there wisdom may be gathered. Whatever experience may know, or enjoyment appropriate, that memory will lay by in store forever. Unlike earth, there is there no duty to self, it is absorbed and satisfied in a higher law of universal love to all others; for self, is only felicity and congratulation.

Toward Trinity are the most all-absorbing dispositions and attractions. There is to Him eternal love; souls filled full of love: love pressed down and running over: love in the majestic, burning presence of the throne: ardent, eternal love. The limited sparks of earth now flaming into bright, warm fires of immortal love to God the Father, the Blessed Son and the Holy Ghost. It kindles into activity; and comprehenson and enjoyment become expressive. Hence the praise, the holy worship, the songs of immortality, the harmony that tunes heaven into one ceaseless holiday of joy and praise. But the language, the chorus, the hopes, the holy refrains of those nearest the throne, the jubilee of the entire host, no one can describe. The resultant obedience which delights to do the will of GOD, the hurrying messengers that fly at the Divine command to do errands of mercy or love to some distant fallen race, are too beatific for our comprehension. The tenderness of an angel's or a glorified saint's love is GOD's love reflected. Such bliss has no end. Eternity, Eternity, Eternity, around, above, beneath, within, shall reign forever!

"What are these arrayed in white robes, and whence come they?" "These are they which came out of great tribulation, and have washed their robes and made them white in the blood of the LAMB." We saw them at toil; we traced them from the heart of sin into penitence and the new birth, through probation's labor, through death's dominion, past the trying ordeal of the resurrection and the judgment. And now, "These are they," the very ones we lost once, in "the valley and shadow:" they emerged from the shadows;

now they are the consolidated family of saints and angels at their eternal home.

Beyond these puny words and dull conceptions is the Christian's peaceful rest. The description is unsatisfying, for we look through a glass darkly. In the light of eternity, in the presence of our elder brothers, the angels, in the cavernous, sepulchral warnings of the lost, we read the destiny of mortal. Perish the body must, perish the soul may, but eternity pivots the momentous results on the present moments. The family circle of GOD would be broken forever by the absence of a lost soul.

CHAPTER VI.

Conclusion.

INFIDELTY is darkness, while God is light, and his word is a lamp. Our creed then is: *The most economical and peaceable way to banish darkness is to light this lamp and the achievement is done.* Such has been our aim in the preceding pages.

When John, in prison, sent to inquire whether Christ were the true Messiah, this divine Logician did not enter into an elaborate argument to prove his divinity, but simply sent a beam of truth into John's dungeon: "Go and show John again those things which ye do hear and see; the blind receive their sight, and the lame walk, the lepers are cleansed, and the deaf hear, the dead are raised up, and the poor have the gospel preached to them."

"And blessed is *he*, whosoever shall not be offended in me."

How potent was this argument, as a two-edged sword of peace! It was sharper than Peter's sword of violence, which cut off the hearing ear of a servant.

Infidelity invents specious theories, ornaments them with silvery eloquence, gives them apparent authority by the rational employment of scientific truth in the premises, obscures the imposing superstructure with voluminous erudition, and while the unwary mind is captivated, nay entranced, by the splendid exhibition, the irrelevant and foreign conclusion is dexterously capped upon the superstructure, high up in the mists of air; and upon that cap is written with concealed pen of infidel, "There is no God." Babel once fell. So must infidelity yield. The old, old story from the heart of God, through the heart of man sanctified, clad in truth, however simple, is All-power incarnate. The decree proclaims: "*My Words shall not pass away.*" Infidelity shall die and melt

"Into air, into thin air;
And, like the baseless fabric of its vision,
Its cloud-capped towers, its gorgeous palaces,

Its solemn temples. * * * *
  Yea, all which it inherit, shall dissolve;
And, like an insubstantial pageant faded,
  Leave not a rack behind; It is such stuff
As dreams are made of."

The great mystery of Godliness reaching up into Heaven and out into the universe, cannot be unraveled in a volume, nor in a generation, nor in a world full of books, nor in time, nor even in eternity. It is the province of infidelity to transform mystery into obscurity, or render it wholly invisible as Aeneas was to Queen Dido.

Eternal truth presented in simple forms, answers all angular cavils. God himself pleads in his works, and I believe God again argues in his Natural Government, and faith rises higher. Then He unfolds His Moral Government, and conviction sinks deeper. Then He incorporates Revelation, and the compounded evidence is incontrovertible. Then He instills the Witness of the Spirit, and the divine evidence buoys up the faith as if on the bosom of a flood. Finally He sends down Answer to Prayer, and the demonstration of his existence fills all space, and the rapt, worshiping soul exclaims: I *know* there is one God, the Creator, the

NATURAL and MORAL GOVERNOR, the REVELATOR, the GREAT WITNESS, the COMMUNING GOD. Then by the same evidence, I know the Bible is His Word and will. What this Revelation of me and relation to me, may be, follows as the weightiest problem of existence? And the Word utters the clear response; "We also are his offspring," by creation, and believing ones by adoption, into a great spiritual family. They live and move in Him, labor and love on His footstool, in death rest in His CHRIST, awake by and by into His immortality, join His Church triumphant, and live with this FATHER-GOD in Heaven, during eternal ages.

APPENDIX.

THE Family Father is GOD. He is not the God of the Veda Bible of the Hindu, for that is a system of Pantheism, in which Brahm becomes Brama by development of wakefulness. He is not of the Sankhya of India, which is a Dualism, admitting two gods, one good, the other evil. He is not of the Nyaya in the Kanada, for that is a doctrine of atoms, synthetically coming together to form a god. This is the same doctrine as that of Epicurus, of Huxley, of Darwin and especially of Leibnitz. This is the original materialism or Pantheism. Our GOD is not the divine of Tao-Tsau, or of Confucius who believed in original monads or atoms. He is not the Zendavesta of Zoroaster, for that is a dualism having a good God of light and of fire and a bad one of darkness.

He does not rise out of Egypt's theory which makes their dualistic god the result of many emanations.

He does not develop from Chaldea's creed which is blind on rigid materialism and fatalism.

God does not emerge from the many phases of Greek Theology, for its every part had been fashioned in thought by India centuries before. The Greek formulas were substantially a rehash. Stoicism, Skepticism, Epicurianism as taught by Epicurus, Pythagoras, Aristotle, Socrates and Plato were merely human philosophies borrowed chiefly from India, yet degenerated from their vigorous thought.

God is not found in Gnosticism, a curious mixture from India, Greece and Persia. He is not in Manicheism which strives to reconcile every other system with Christianity. He is not in Arabian philosophy which compounds human reason and infinite intelligence.

While truth shines brighter and brighter unto the perfect day, on the other hand, error is more deformed and obnoxious as it takes on new shapes. Hence all modern creeds of error, though only transfers from antiquity, have lost freshness and vigor. There is nothing clearer to him who will read and compare the old with the new, than that all these modern skepticisms, infidelities and new departures, are simply a new morphology of what long ago was formulated for pastime among the heathen. India is the father of all infidelities, though they all deny it as an unpopular parentage.

Our God therefore has no modern origin. The notion of Him is not derived from Hobbs in whose Social Materialism his only God is sense; nor from D'Holback whose theory was Sensual Materialism: nor from Hume who floundered in Skeptical Sensualism; nor from Spinoza who revived old Material Pantheism; nor from Descartes who is lost in Speculative Rationalism; nor from the Platonism of Henry Moore who said, immutable space was the only God; nor from the Idealism of Leibnitz who starts every existing thing from the monad; nor from Volney who is the grossest of Sensualists, wholly denying God; nor from Darwin, Huxley, Spencer, nor Strauss, for they are not original. They have robbed the philosophical graves of the Orient. They have borrowed old thoughts without credit and call them new. We cannot respect their ingenuity in attempting to conceal the fraud.

We *do* derive our certain ideas of God from the Bible. Here we start. Here alone is the theory of miracles confirmed even by heathen writers. Here is perfect harmony, wisdom, light and satisfaction.

The Bible's God is confirmed in nature, in science, in moral government, in natural government, in Providence, in grace, and by the "Witness of the Spirit."

This is the only God whose religion ever tended

to civilization, or liberty, or female equality, or individual accountability, or national integrity, or financial prosperity, or universal brotherhood, or love to enemies.

This is our God. He is the Father of the Christian family. He is the Head of the Christian Church.

www.ingramcontent.com/pod-product-compliance
Lightning Source LLC
LaVergne TN
LVHW010235110826
845151LV00004B/1305

* 9 7 8 1 4 2 5 5 2 4 9 8 2 *